CALVIN
CELEBRATED

THE GENEVAN REFORMER
AND HIS HUGUENOT SONS

A Contribution to the
John Calvin Quincentenary
1509–2009

Reprinted to Commemorate the 450th Anniversary
of the St Bartholomew Massacre (1572)

Alan C. Clifford

CHARENTON REFORMED PUBLISHING
2009

First published in Great Britain 2009 by Charenton Reformed Publishing

www.christiancharenton.co.uk

Reprinted 2022

ISBN 978–0–9555165–3–5

Typeset in Bembo MT Pro 11 on 13 point

Typeset in Great Britain by Quinta Press, Weston Rhyn

British Library Cataloguing in Publication Data.

A catalogue record for this book is available from the British Library.

Cover concept: the Author, executed by Barkers Print & Design Ltd, Attleborough, Norfolk

NOTE TO THE READER

In order to achieve maximum impact, without the distraction of detailed footnotes, the original was intended as a semi-popular text. This has been retained unaltered. However, for those who wish to explore the subject further, adequate 'further reading' lists appear at the end of each chapter.

THE AUTHOR

Dr Alan Clifford (b. 1941) hails from Farnborough, Hampshire. Reared in Methodism and converted in Anglicanism (1958), he embraced Puritanism through the influence of Dr D. Martyn Lloyd-Jones (1963). An engineering career at the Royal Aircraft Establishment and the RAF Institute of Aviation Medicine, Farnborough (1958–66) was terminated after God's call to pastoral ministry. This led to university study (University of Wales, Bangor, 1966–69) and eventual ordination to the Congregational ministry (1969). He remains (since 1988) a minister without-charge of the Presbyterian Church of Wales. Now retired, Alan pursued pastoral ministry in Northampton, Gateshead, Great Ellingham, Norfolk, and Norwich. Academic profile: BA (philosophy) 1969; MLitt (philosophy of religion) 1978; PhD (historical theology) 1983. An in-depth study of Arminianism and Calvinism, Dr Clifford's doctoral thesis was published by Oxford University Press in 1990. Author of several books (and a few hymns) on this and related themes include Philip Doddridge, the present work and Welsh Calvinistic Methodism. Richard Baxter and Dr Edmund Calamy have occupied his attention in recent years.

To the Memory of
VICTOR BUDGEN
(1937–89)
Faithful Pastor & Church Historian
whose Huguenot book collection I inherited
through the kindness of his devoted widow Pauline.

Acknowledgements

For the type-setting, layout and production of this book I am grateful for the personal interest and professional expertise of Dr Digby James of Quinta Press. Barkers Print & Design are thanked for help with formatting the cover, and the facilities provided by Lightning Source are much appreciated.

Besides the constant support of my loving wife Marian, others deserve my warmest appreciation. Ever since discovering Huguenot history in 1985, many friends from Norfolk and elsewhere have encouraged my interest and shared my enthusiasm for the French Reformed legacy. Without their kind support, visits to France (1989, 1991, 2008) and Geneva (2007, 2009) would not have been made. I am especially grateful to our son Dr Hywel Clifford for arranging a most memorable visit to Saumur in September 2008. These various influences explain this historical *hors d'oeuvre*, first published in 2009. I trust this reprint encourages others to explore the awesome and inspiring riches of the Huguenot epic.

SOLI DEO GLORIA

CONTENTS

CALVIN COMMENDATIONS

JAMES ARMINIUS (1560–1609): "I affirm that [Calvin] excels beyond comparison in the true interpretation of Scripture, and that his commentaries ought to be more highly valued than all that is handed down to us by the library of the Fathers."

MOSES AMYRAUT (1596–1664): "That incomparable Calvin, to whom mainly, next to God, the Church owes its Reformation, not only in France, but in many other parts of Europe. The excellencies of a very distinguished man, his manifestly herculean toils undertaken and endured for the sake of truth, and his invaluable services to the Church of our Lord Jesus in the last century, appear not only to entreat but to demand from us, that we shall protect his memory with extraordinary zeal against the reproaches of adversaries."

RICHARD BAXTER (1615–1691): "I know no man, since the Apostles' days, whom I value and honour more than Calvin, and whose judgment in all things, one with another, I more esteem and come nearer to."

PHILIP DODDRIDGE (1702–1751): "Calvin has a multitude of judicious thoughts."

JOHN WESLEY (1703–91): "I believe Calvin was a great instrument of God; and that he was a wise and pious man."

CHARLES H. SPURGEON (1834–92): "Calvin, after all, knew more about the gospel than almost any man who has ever lived, uninspired..."

Introduction

Born at Noyon in Picardy, John Calvin (1509–64) is generally regarded as the most eminent of the Protestant reformers of the sixteenth century. Exiled from his native France, he became a pastor of the Church of Geneva and the organizing genius of the Protestant Reformation. While his Christ-exalting influence as a theologian, preacher and commentator became—and remains—truly international, Calvin's labours were particularly fruitful in France. His spirituality also found expression in the *Confession of Faith* and presbyterian *Discipline* of the French Reformed churches drawn up at the first National Synod held at Paris in 1559. Through the zealous evangelistic labours of pastors trained in Geneva, around 2,000 churches had been founded by 1560. Yet Huguenot piety was to be constantly tested through nearly three centuries of fierce persecution including the terrible St Bartholomew massacre of August 24, 1572. Cruelly harassed by the Roman Church, the noble army of French Reformed martyrs never failed to demonstrate the grace, electing love and faithfulness of the living God. Thus John Calvin's Bible-based, God-honouring legacy was constantly vindicated in the most inspiring epic of faith and fortitude ever known.

In the reign of Henri IV, the Edict of Nantes (1598) provided a fragile and frequently violated peace. Directed by the Jesuits, the Roman Church pursued a policy of cruel extermination. This tolerant Edict was finally revoked by the despotic Louis XIV in 1685. Huguenot temples were demolished and the flocks were scattered. The faithful worshipped in woods and caves and other remote places; their assemblies were known as the 'churches of the desert'. Those captured by the dragoons were punished. Pastors, elders and others were either hanged or sent to the galleys. The women were sent to prison and the children re-educated in Jesuit schools. Many emigrated to Holland, Germany, Great Britain and elsewhere. The frustrations and sufferings of those who remained led to the tragic Camisard war of 1702–9. But God did not forsake his covenant people. Under the inspired leadership of Antoine Court (*1696–1760*) and Paul Rabaut (*1718–94*), there was an amazing revival of the Reformed churches, beginning in the remote southern province of Languedoc.

The persecutions gradually eased. The last Huguenot galley slaves were released in 1775. At last, with public opinion beginning to change, the Edict of Toleration was granted in 1787 on the eve of the French Revolution. The diabolical tyranny of the Vatican-backed French monarchs received its just reward in the terror and bloodshed of the revolution (1789). It was a miracle that French Protestantism ever survived. Yet, in the midst of indescribable suffering, the testimony of the Huguenot pastors and people alike was unshaken. In their faithful witness to our Lord Jesus Christ, the assurance of the psalmist was theirs too: 'Blessed be the Lord, who daily loads us with benefits, even the God of our salvation… O God, You are terrible out of Your holy places: the God of Israel is he that gives strength and power unto his people. Blessed be God' (*Psalm 68:19, 35*).

While Calvin's life and achievements are well known, the events and personalities of the French Reformation are mostly unknown, at least to the general Christian public. This is unfortunate since Calvin's influence on later generations of French Protestants is a truly fascinating and inspiring story. In addition to the main chapter on Calvin, the outlines of five eminent Huguenot pastors—not to ignore a little-known 'English son'—are presented to raise the profile of these and other servants of Christ whose dedicated labours for the Gospel deserve to be better known. In days of unparallelled apostasy and confusion within the professing Church, these Huguenot heroes challenge us to greater faithfulness and dedication to the cause of Christ. If this quincentenary celebration contributes to that end then the author's enthusiasm for his subject will have been justified.

I

John Calvin

I

While Calvin is forever associated with Geneva, he was of course a Frenchman. Exiled from his native land, he became a pastor of the Church of Geneva and the organizing genius of the Protestant Reformation. As such, he heralded the most consistent return to the Bible of all the reformers of the sixteenth century, augmenting and consolidating the work done by Luther and Zwingli before him. To make a claim about his significance (despite all the vitriolic criticisms by his enemies and detractors), he is arguably the greatest Christian theologian of all time. Indeed, he was the Paul of the Reformation. As we shall see, this is no idle boast. His successor Theodore Beza affirmed of Calvin: 'No theologian of this period (I do not speak invidiously) wrote more purely, weightily, and judiciously, though he wrote more than any individual in our recollection or that of our fathers.'

Calvin the Huguenot

Personifying all the features of the Huguenots, Calvin may therefore be regarded as their 'prototype.' As such, while his Christ-exalting influence as a theologian, preacher and commentator was truly international, Calvin's labours found full and fruitful expression in France. The comprehensive and clear Scriptural dynamism of the *Institutes of the Christian Religion*, the majesty and tenderness of the Genevan *Psalter*, the simplicity and reverence of the reformed *Liturgy* and the practical directness of the *Catechism* gave the French Reformed churches a unique, powerful and godly character. As

9

noted in the introduction, Calvin's spirituality also found expression in the *Confession of Faith* and presbyterian *Discipline* of the French Reformed churches drawn up at the first National Synod held at Paris in 1559. His exile notwithstanding, this godly genius could hardly have had greater influence had he stayed in France. Denied the joys of human fatherhood (judged by his cruel critics as a sign of divine displeasure), Calvin's bold and prophetic response is famous: 'My sons are to be found all over the world.' However, this was not only true in his own day. Indeed, he had 'sons' in successive generations of whom it may be said that they too embraced Calvin's deeply-devotional and passionate piety. This was expressed in his motto, 'I offer my heart to God as a sacrifice', words used in a letter to his 'bosom brother', Guillaume Farel in 1540. Calvin illustrated them by a hand holding a heart heavenwards, beneath which appear the Latin words: *prompte et sincere*—'willing and true' (in the work of the Lord).

Birth and early education

In view of the constant succession of Calvin biographies from the sixteenth century to the present day (Beza's first appeared in 1564, his second in 1575), we shall not provide an exhaustive account of the life of Jean Cauvin (Latinised to Calvinus, hence Calvin). However, an attempt will be made to explore the rare individuality of this man, born 'in the shadow of the cathedral' at Noyon in Picardy on 10 July 1509. His father Gérard was an important ecclesiastical administrator. John was one of nine children, his father having married twice. At the age of fourteen, Calvin went to study in Paris, first at the Collège de la Marche, then at the Collège Montaigu. At the first institution he was taught Latin by the famous teacher Mathurin Cordier. A brilliant and disciplined student, Calvin's persistent application to study contributed to his later ill-health. The second institution was a kind of 'educational monastery' in which the pupils were expected to engage in confession of sins and mutual rebuke. Young Calvin was so conscientious in the latter that his fellow students nicknamed him 'the accusative case'!

At first, Gérard wished his son to enter the priesthood, but since

the legal profession offered better prospects, Calvin went obediently
to Orleans to study law. Here in 1528 he met the German Lutheran
scholar Melchoir Wolmar who had a great and lasting influence
on Calvin, both in presenting the Gospel to him and urging the
young man to dedicate his great talents to the Gospel. Boarding
in Wolmar's house at this time was another significant individual,
nine-year old Theodore de Bèze (or Beza), the future reformer's
successor in Geneva. Among the professors of the University of
Orleans during this period was Nicolas Bérauld, the teacher of
the future Huguenot leader Gaspard de Coligny and his brothers.
Having progressed through the usual academic gradations, here
(at the end of a second period) Calvin probably took his licentiate
in 1531, receiving his doctorate soon after, as was the custom.

Calvin's character

Perhaps less dramatic than the careers of Luther and Zwingli,
Calvin's involved a more introverted personality. While Luther
was 'bold', yet not averse to periods of deep depression, Calvin
acknowledged himself to be 'naturally timid and fearful' although
he could be lion-like in the cause of Christ. Despite deep hostility
to all things Protestant, an early Catholic writer, Florimond de
Raemond gives us a glimpse of Calvin in his student days: 'In a
lean, worn body his mind was ever alive and vigorous, prompt in
repartee, bold in attack. He fasted much, even in his youth, either
for his health's sake to stop the mental haze of migraines which
afflicted him continually, or to gain for his mind more freedom to
write, study and to improve his memory. ... He spoke but little.
Nothing but serious remarks and remarks which went home. He
was never seen amongst groups of his fellows, always retiring, of a
melancholy disposition. ... sharing his thoughts with few people,
not taking pleasure in any company other than that of his own
thoughts, a lover of seclusion.'

Despite some evidence of unsympathetic bias here, we get an idea
of Calvin's personality. Less objectively, Florimond de Raemond
blames Wolmar for giving Calvin his 'taste for heresy.' Following
him from Orleans to the University of Bourges (Wolmar was invited

to teach Greek there by Marguerite de Navarre), Calvin benefited further from this 'heretical' influence. It is plain that the Lutheran saw immense intellectual, literary and religious potential in his young friend whose company he obviously enjoyed. In later years, Calvin dedicated his commentary on 2 Corinthians to Wolmar who, in 1546, responded by sending the author a silver cup.

Evangelical conversion

Ever a dutiful son, Calvin hastened home to Noyon during his father's last and fatal illness in 1531. Later that year, he became greatly influenced by the new humanistic learning, eventually publishing a commentary on the Roman philosopher Seneca's *De Clementia* in 1532. Besides showing himself a highly competent classicist, it is thought that Calvin was employing this means to arouse clemency in the King towards the persecuted evangelicals. Demonstrating evidence of the Holy Spirit's influence in Calvin's life, that same year saw him engaged in evangelical preaching at Bourges. Calvin's involvement with Nicolas Cop's rectoral sermon on 1 November 1533 certainly suggests that he experienced his 'evangelical conversion' around this time (although some uncertainty exists about the precise date). Whenever it occurred, the details of Calvin's amazing conversion were later revealed in the preface to his *Commentary on the Psalms* (1557). Here we make a further discovery of Calvin's personality. Whatever his critics have said regarding an allegedly frigid and logical disposition, an extraordinary emotional quality emerged when he met God in Christ for the first time:

> Even while I was a boy my father had destined me for theology; then, later, as he considered that the knowledge of law commonly enriched those who followed it, this hope made him straightway change his mind. This, then, was why I was taken from the study of philosophy and put to learn law, from which (although I made every effort to use my talents faithfully in obedience to my father) nevertheless God in His secret providence finally curbed and turned me in another direction. At first, although I was so obstinately given to the superstitions of the papacy, that it was extremely difficult to drag me from the depths of the mire, yet by a sudden conversion He tamed my heart and made it teachable, this heart which for its age was excessively hardened in such

matters. So, having received some taste and knowledge of true piety, I was at once inflamed with so great a desire to advance that, although I did not entirely leave my other studies, yet nevertheless I was less rigorous in the way I devoted myself to them.

Whatever may be said about the cold and clinical character of many who claim Calvin's name, this remarkable testimony should be sufficient to dispel the impression that Calvinism's founder fathered a sour spirituality. Every bit as colourful as Luther's account of his own conversion, Calvin revealed more of himself, albeit in a self-effacing prayer to the Lord, in his *Letter to Cardinal Sadolet* (1539):

> Every time that I looked within myself, or raised my heart to Thee, so violent a horror overtook me that there were neither purifications nor satisfactions which could in any way cure me. The more I gazed at myself the sharper were the pricks which pressed my conscience, to such a point that there remained no other solace or comfort than to deceive myself by forgetting myself. ...

Then, acknowledging a stubborn persistence in Rome's superstitious and ritualistic piety (prior to his discovery of evangelical truth), and realising after considerable personal struggle that this 'different form of doctrine' was not alien to a true 'Christian profession', Calvin concludes:

> ... I began to understand, as if someone had brought me a light, in what mire of error I had wallowed, and had become filthy, and with how much mud and dirt I had been defiled. Being then grievously troubled and distracted, as was my duty, on account of the knowledge of the eternal death which hung over me, I judged nothing more necessary to me after having condemned with groaning and tears my past manner of life, than to give myself up and to betake myself to Thy way. ...'

Escaping persecution

King Francis I's increasing hostility towards evangelicals, together with the anger of the Parlement of Paris against Cop, also threatened Calvin—a possible contributor to the 'heretical' address. Leaping through a window disguised as a vine-dresser, he escaped from Paris, returning to Noyon before going to Saintonge. He was then invited by his friend Louis du Tillet—parish priest at Claix and canon of the cathedral—to move to Angoulême. Here, for several

months, in safety and seclusion, Calvin welcomed the opportunity
to continue his studies. With no grand designs for public service,
Calvin's account of this time (written later from Orleans) reveals
a deepening spirituality:

> I should consider myself very happy if I am allowed to spend this
> time of exile or retreat in such tranquillity. But the Lord will do what
> pleases Him, His providence will see what is best. I have learned by
> experience that we are not allowed to see too much of the future.
> While I was promising myself that I would be quiet, the danger of
> which I had no fear at all was at the gates [he was sought for in the
> Collège Fortet in Paris]. And on the other hand, when I feared that
> my stay would be a frightful one, a nest has been prepared for me in
> quietness, contrary to all expectation, and it is the hand of God that
> has done all this. If we trust in Him, He will watch over us Himself.

Angoulême and the Institutes

Vital for the entire future course of the Reformation, Calvin's
immortal masterpiece -his *Institutes of the Christian Religion*—was
conceived during his solitude at Angoulême. The eventual impact
of this work is revealed by the predictable animosity of Florimond
de Raemond: 'Angoulême was the forge in which this new Vulcan
fashioned on the anvil the strange opinions which he has since
published. For it was there, to surprise Christendom, he first
wove the tapestry of his *Institutes*, this book that one may call the
Qur'an or rather the *Talmud* of heresy.' Indeed, this was a work
no one could ignore!

In April 1534, we find Calvin at Nérac, the little capital of Albret
in which the King's sister, Marguerite of Angoulême—Queen
of Navarre and mother of Jeanne d'Albret—gave succour and
encouragement to persecuted evangelicals. As we have seen, the
Queen was eminent for evangelical piety. We may be sure that
twenty-five year old Calvin would have met the eighty-year old
pioneer of French Protestantism, Jacques Lefèvre d'Etaples, for
some years a permanent guest of Marguerite. He never openly
broke with Rome as young Calvin was shortly to do (by resigning
certain benefices he enjoyed). In fact, it grieved the old man that
while his ground-breaking labours had led many to martyrdom,

he himself always lacked the courage they displayed in their heroic sufferings.

Later that year, Calvin was developing contacts destined to play a significant part in his life. For instance, he wrote to Martin Bucer, the reformer at Strasbourg, and whom he hoped to meet. Again in Paris, he planned a meeting with a notorious young Spanish doctor, Michael Servetus, who had recently published a small book attacking the Trinity (*De Erroribus Trinitatis*, 1531). Sadly, Servetus did not honour the appointment. Had he done so, Calvin might very well have rescued him from his Arian heresy, avoiding in the process a future execution that has left a stain on Calvin's reputation to this day—of which more anon.

The Mass repudiated

Moving on, Calvin went to Poitiers, where a group of evangelical friends gathered around him. Among many subjects they discussed was one of the central questions of the Reformation, that of the Mass and the real presence of Christ. Apparently, a local cave or grotto was the scene where these brethren celebrated the very first Reformed Lord's Supper. Calvin clarified their understanding when, according to Florimond de Raemond:

> Calvin having his Bible before him said, "Here is my Mass." And, throwing the hood of his cloak on to the table and raising his eyes to heaven, he exclaimed, "Lord, if on the day of judgement you hold it against me that I never went to mass and that I left it, I shall say and with reason, Lord, you did not command it. Here is your law, here is Scripture which is the rule you have given me, in which I have not been able to find any sacrifice other than that which was offered on the altar of the cross.

The significance of all this cannot be questioned. As the papal decree *Dominus Iesus* (2000) has made clear in recent times, that 'ecclesial communities' without the priesthood and sacraments of Rome cannot be regarded as churches 'in any proper sense', Calvin and his brethren were cutting themselves off from Christ and the means of grace if Rome's case is valid. However, thoroughly grasping the teaching of the Epistle to the Hebrews and perceiving the philosophical fiction of transubstantiation, they were sure of their ground in rejecting the blasphemies of the Mass.

First theological writing

The year 1534 is significant for another reason, the writing of Calvin's first theological treatise, *Psychopannychia* (a word meaning 'the watch of souls'). Despite the urgency felt by the author, the work was not published for several years, first in Latin (1542) and later in French (1558). Heralding his first response to the disruptive and revolutionary Anabaptist movement, Calvin was anxious to show that the authentic movement of Bible-based reform must not be confused with these fanatics. The subject of the treatise was the Anabaptist theory of 'soul sleep', that after death, the soul 'sleeps' until the day of judgement since it cannot exist apart from the body until the resurrection of the whole man. Concerned initially to avoid needless dispute, the increasing popularity of this teaching drew Calvin to deal with it. By means of careful biblical study, he conclusively demonstrated that our immortal souls live after they have left the body (see *Matt. 10:28; Lk. 23:43; Phil. 1:21; Heb. 12:23; Rev. 6:9*).

The Institutes published

Towards the end of the year 1534, their lives being in constant danger, Calvin and his friend Louis du Tillet made their way to Basle via Strasbourg. Despite the frustrating theft of some of their money near Metz, Almighty God was clearly leading his servant in the cause of recovering the true Gospel of our Lord Jesus Christ. Settled in Basle, Calvin became quietly occupied in preparing his masterpiece for the press, the *Institution de la religion chrétienne*. However, an event occurred in France to hasten the book's publication—the 'affair of the placards'—in which the Mass was vigorously denounced all over Paris, a copy of the protest even appearing on the door of the King's bed chamber! This highly-provocative protest created a cruel backlash of persecution. For all its boldness, Calvin was concerned with the consequences of the action for the cause of the Gospel. He later wrote, 'On the occasion of the placards, fury flared up so greatly against the faithful that our cause was made odious.' The King, grouping the placardists with the revolutionary and seditious Anabaptists, had no time for careful discrimination between straightforward religious protest and political opportunism. These developments drove Calvin to publish his work sooner than he had planned. In the circumstances, he 'dare not remain silent', as he later made clear:

And this was the reason which spurred me on to publish my *Institutes of the Christian Religion.* Firstly, in order to reply to these evil charges which others were sowing and to clear my brothers whose death was precious before the Lord. Then afterwards, in so far as the same cruelties might soon be practised against many other poor people, so that foreign nations should be at least touched with some compassion and care for them. For I did not produce the book as it is now [1557], a thorough treatment and the result of great toil. It was then only a little booklet containing in summary the principal matters, and it had no other object but that people should be informed what faith was held by those whom I could see evil and lawless flatterers were vilifying in a foul and most mischievous way.

One smiles at Calvin's description of the first edition of the *Institutes*! His 'little booklet'—based on the Ten Commandments, The Apostles' Creed and the Lord's Prayer—ran to 519 pages, even though it was easily slipped beneath one's cloak. Eventually printed in Basle in March 1536, the work was dedicated to Francis I. The conspicuously-loyal 'epistle dedicatory' is itself a 'plea for the persecuted evangelicals.' Even then, the 'timid and fearful' author's dedication boldly defended Gospel truth in the clearest and purest terms, punctuated throughout with scriptural language:

Before God we are miserable sinners: in men's eyes most despised—if you will, the offscouring and refuse of the world, or anything viler that can be named. Thus, before God nothing remains for us to boast of, save his mercy alone, whereby we have been saved through no merit of our own: and before men nothing but our weakness, which even to admit is to them the greatest dishonour. But our doctrine must tower unvanquished above all the glory and above all the might of the world, for it is not of us, but of the living God and his Christ whom the Father has appointed King to 'rule from sea to sea, and from the rivers even to the ends of the earth.' And he is so to rule as to smite the whole earth with its iron and brazen strength, with its gold and silver brilliance, shattering it with the rod of his mouth as earthen vessels, just as the prophets have prophesied concerning the magnificence of his reign. Indeed, our adversaries cry out that we falsely make the Word of God our pretext, and wickedly corrupt it. By reading our confession you can judge according to your prudence not only how malicious a calumny but also what utter effrontery this is.

This one extract sets the tone for the entire Huguenot epic, as it was to unfold during the next three centuries. Sad to say, there is no evidence that Francis ever read the work. Indeed, although they were determined to make their witness before all the world, the reformers were not deceived about their prospects of success with the rulers of the earth. Henry Bullinger wrote accurately to Martin Bucer: 'I do not know what good we can expect from the King of France; he is a godless and ambitious debauchee.'

Respite in Italy

Shortly after the book's publication, Calvin and his friend Louis du Tillet travelled to Italy. They spent a short time at the court of Renée, Duchess of Ferrara, who had expressed a desire to meet Calvin. Sharing the same evangelical convictions, this godly lady was on intimate terms with her cousin, Marguerite de Navarre. Daughter of Louis XII, Renée of France would have been Queen had it not been for the Salic Law which excluded women from the throne of France. Married to Hercule d'Este, Duke of Ferrara (son of Lucretia Borgia), Renée was even more open than Marguerite in her attachment to the new teaching. Welcoming evangelical scholars (including the poet Clément Marot in 1535), what Nérac and the court of Marguerite de Navarre were in France, Ferrara was in Italy around the zealous and cultured Duchess. Her husband did not share her enthusiastic support for the likes of Calvin (who, for 'security' reasons, used his pseudonymn during his time at Ferrara—Charles d'Espeville). When reproached by the Duke for supporting the exiled evangelicals, the indignant Renée would reply, "What do you expect me to do? They are poor French folk of my own nation, who would now be my subjects if God had given me a beard on my chin and I had been a man!" Indeed, how different the history of France, Europe and the world might have been, if France had had a Protestant queen?

After Marot and other evangelicals met with persecution at Ferrara in the spring of 1536, Calvin considered it wise to move on. Conversations with Renée had made a favourable impression on him, judging by a letter he later wrote to her (from Basle or Paris). This letter also reveals the writer's maturing piety:

> I recognised in you such fear of God and such a faithful desire to obey Him that even apart from the lofty station which he has given you amongst men I have a high regard for the graces that He has placed in you, so that I should think myself accursed if I missed occasion to serve you. This I say without any flattery or pretence but in sincerity of heart and speaking as before Him to whom all our secret thoughts are open.

Against the background of those who, like Renée's chaplain, took a low 'Nicodemite' profile regarding the Roman mass while sympathising with evangelical ideas, Calvin—in his letter to the Duchess—explained why compromise was unthinkable. If he questioned the methods of the Paris placardists, Calvin shared their concern to champion the cause of Christ on this basic issue of the Reformation:

> In so far as the mass is a sacrifice ordained by men for the redemption and salvation of the living and the dead, as their canon states, it is an intolerable blasphemy in which the sufferings of Jesus Christ are overthrown as if they were of no avail. For what we assert—that the faithful [believers] have been redeemed by the blood of Jesus and have obtained through Him the remission of their sins, righteousness and the hope of eternal life—that must be understood in so far as this loving Saviour, by offering Himself to the Father and by giving Himself up to be killed, offered Himself as an eternal sacrifice through which our iniquities have been purged and cleansed and we ourselves received into the grace of the Father and become partakers of the heavenly inheritance, as the apostle unfolds at sufficient length in the Epistle to the Hebrews. If, therefore, the death of Jesus is not recognized as a unique sacrifice made once and for all in order that it might possess an eternal virtue, what remains for the sacrifice but to be wiped out as if it were of no avail? I know quite well that, to cover their abomination, these liars say that they perform the same sacrifice that Jesus made. But thence arise several blasphemies. For

this sacrifice could be made only by Himself, and the apostle says that if He is now being sacrificed, He must now still be suffering. Consequently, you can see that one or the other must be true: either we must recognize the horrible blasphemy of the mass and detest it, or by approving it we must trample under foot the cross of Jesus. How different and opposed this is to the Supper of Christ I leave you to consider for yourself after having read in the Holy Scriptures of the institution of this Supper. But the great abomination which is committed is the idolatry that is made in it, a creature being adored in the place of God, which is quite inexcusable.

II

The road to Geneva

After selling his estate at Noyon, Calvin set off towards Strasbourg with his brother and sister, determined to pursue his theological work in peace. This was a major turning point in Calvin's life. He was leaving France never to return. Despite his plans for a quiet life, the providence of God was planning a very different career for him. The road to Strasbourg was barred due to warfare in eastern France, so the exiles made a detour via Lyons and Geneva. Who can best tell what happened next but Calvin himself? He revealed this astonishing account in his *Commentary on the Psalms* (1557):

Master Guillaume Farel held me back in Geneva, not so much by his advice and urgent exhortation as by a fearsome adjuration, as if God from on high had stretched out His hand upon me to stay me. As the most direct road to Strasbourg, whither I wished at that time to retire, was closed by warfare I had decided to slip through Geneva without stopping more than one night in the town. Now a short time previously, popery had been thrown out through the instrumentality of this good person above mentioned [Farel] and by Pierre Viret. But things had not yet settled, and there were divisions and evil and dangerous factions amongst the townsfolk. Then a certain person (who has now most evilly revolted and returned to the papists) [probably Du Tillet who left Calvin in 1538] discovered me and told others of my presence. Whereupon Farel, who was burning with a better zeal for the advance of the gospel, straightway made every effort to hold me back. Now after he heard that I had some particular study for which I wished to keep myself free, when he saw that he could get nowhere by prayer he even went as far as a curse, that it might please God to curse my rest and the tranquillity for study that I was seeking if in so great a necessity I were to withdraw and refuse to give my help and assistance. This word frightened me and shattered me so much that I set aside the journey I had planned, yet I remained in my shame and timidity, unwilling to have to take on any definite responsibility.

Such is the testimony of a man claimed and mastered by God, this 'timid and fearful man' who, through grace, was to declare, "I offer my heart to God as a sacrifice"—who was to serve *prompte et sincere* in the work of the Lord. This amazing event explains why Calvin's name is forever associated with the city of Geneva.

The Genevan reformers

For all Calvin's eminence, he was but one instrument in that cause of God known as the Protestant Reformation, a fact he humbly acknowledged. Having already noticed Farel and, in Calvin's testimony, Pierre Viret (who served alongside Calvin from 1559–61), Beza's comparison of the complementary talents of the Genevan trio is noteworthy: 'It was a most pleasing spectacle to see and hear those three distinguished men, carrying on the work of God so harmoniously, and yet differing so much from each other in the nature of their gifts. Farel excelled in a certain sublimity of mind, so that nobody could either hear his thunders without trembling, or listen to his most fervent prayers without feeling almost as it were carried up into heaven. Viret possessed such winning eloquence, that his entranced audience hung upon his lips. Calvin never spoke without filling the mind of the hearer with most weighty sentiments. I have often thought that a preacher compounded of the three would have been absolutely perfect.'

Farel was indeed famous for his 'thunders.' Having laboured with Briçonnet at Meaux near Paris and at his native Gap in Dauphiné, he escaped persecution in France. Going to Basle, he later ministered in Montbéliard, Lausanne and Neuchatel. Everywhere he went, Farel provoked riots. By 1532 he was arousing crowds in Geneva, his powerful oratory creating antagonism and inviting threats to his life on several occasions. Despite all the tumult and opposition, Farel's zeal for the Gospel had a positive impact. In May 1536, the city councillors and people of Geneva solemnly proclaimed their resolution to live according to the Gospel. However, the dust had hardly settled by the time Calvin arrived in August 1536. Noticing that 'everything was in confusion', Calvin's observation clearly indicated that the Genevan reformation needed direction, organisation and stability. Having performed his necessary role in demolishing the old order, it was Farel's greatness that he recognised in Calvin God's instrument for reconstructing the new.

The Genevan Church Constitution

Calvin's eminence in Geneva developed slowly. Starting as little more than a theological counsellor to Farel, even in 1537 he was simply 'lecturer in Holy Scripture.' However, in various disputes, Calvin was astounding audiences with his familiarity with the church Fathers and his patristic learning. His major impact began when he drew up a document of church reform—*Articles concernant l'organisation de l'église ... à Genève.* These articles covered matters to do with the Lord's Supper, viz. frequency of celebration, avoidance of hypocrisy and the necessity of discipline. Great care was taken over this, not least because the reformers had to replace the Roman mass with an alternative demanding a more sincere personal piety than formerly. Calvin and his brethren had a deeper regard for the sacraments than is perhaps generally the case among many Protestants today. He even desired the Lord's Supper to be celebrated weekly in the three Genevan churches—St. Pierre, Rive and St. Gervais. In this respect, the so-called 'dictator of Geneva' never got his way! Indeed, the city Council insisted on a celebration of the sacrament just four times a year (at Christmas, Easter and Pentecost, and in September), a tradition which still prevails in the Reformed churches of Europe (and Scotland) to this day.

Presbyterian Order and Worship

Reflecting a radical biblical policy of reform, these articles also saw the beginnings of the presbyterian form of church order, where groups of elders (Greek, *presbuteroi*) replaced the authority of priests directed by a single diocesan bishop (episcopacy). At this early stage, however, these elders were appointed by the council rather than the worshipping congregations. Calvin's ideal of a free church within a free state was something for the future, not realised in Calvin's lifetime. The Constitution also prescribed the singing of Psalms, not by trained choirs but by the entire congregation. As we shall see, this provision was to have immense influence on the piety of the Huguenots and other European Reformed churches. Another article stressed the importance of the instruction of the young. Unlike the later 1542 catechism, the initial 1537 catechism was not in the question and answer form, being virtually a summary of Calvin's 1536 *Institutio*. Last of all, a twenty-one article *Confession de la Foy* or 'Confession of Faith' was drawn up requiring personal subscription by the citizens of Geneva.

When the 1537 Articles were approved by the two councils (the Little Council and the Council of the Two Hundred), objections were raised by some of the townsfolk and tensions developed. While Calvin, Farel and their brethren insisted that participation at the Lord's Supper required an acceptance of the confession of faith, the city authorities stated that no citizen should be barred. The issue was fundamental: who has the right to exercise discipline of the Lord's table, the pastors or the politicians?

Crisis and banishment

Matters came to a head early in 1538 when the Council of the Two Hundred voted to conform to the less-rigorous ceremonies of the Church at Berne, demanding too that the Council should regulate church life. Calvin and his brethren opposed this ruling. When the blind pastor Coraud refused to observe a ban on preaching, he was imprisoned. Calvin and Farel protested against this high-handed action. Determined to minister, on Easter Day Calvin preached in St. Pierre and Farel at St. Gervais. But because of the popular disturbance in the city, the preachers refused to hold the communion service which, in their view, would 'profane so holy a mystery.' This faithful resistance won them few friends. To resolve the crisis, the councils met on 23 April. By a majority vote, the pastors were ordered to leave Geneva within three days. Undaunted, 'timid and fearful' Calvin made his famous and courageous reply:

"Right! well and good! If we had served men we should have been ill requited. But we serve a great Master, who will reward us."

At every turn, Calvin's personal wishes were being crossed. Intending to spend only a night in Geneva, his stay extended to eighteen months! Willing to serve the Lord there, he was now banished! On moving to Basle with Farel, again he planned to study quietly, intending to produce another edition of the *Institutes*. When the Strasbourg reformers, Bucer, Capito and Sturm urged Calvin to minister among them, he was again reluctant to respond. However, when Bucer used a Farel-like imprecation to arouse the comfortably-settled scholar, the 'timid and fearful' Calvin again felt the call of God. Moving to Strasbourg, he was soon engaged in pastoring refugees driven out of France by persecution. On Sunday, 8 September 1538 he preached for the first time in the church of St. Nicolas-aux-Ondes.

Strasbourg was an important city in several respects. A cross-roads between France, Germany, Switzerland and the Netherlands, various reforming outlooks—Lutherans, Anabaptists, Zwinglians and French evangelicals—coexisted and interacted under the wise and irenic direction of Martin Bucer. Seventeen years Bucer's junior, Calvin had immense respect for his 'elder brother.' Furthermore, Bucer significantly influenced the younger reformer's thinking on several issues. Having replaced the episcopal system with presbyterian order, Bucer—like Calvin—insisted that such was 'an ordinance given to us by the Holy Spirit Himself' and absolutely necessary for disciplined observance of the Lord's Supper. However, besides reinforcing his conviction that elders should be appointed by the church rather than the state, Calvin learned from Bucer the importance of the four ministries of pastor, teacher, elder and deacon. In the area of worship and liturgy, Calvin also felt the influence of Bucer. As he later acknowledged, 'As for the Sunday prayers I took the form of Strasbourg and borrowed the larger part of it.' In other respects, Calvin did not follow Bucer, not least with regard to literary style. Unlike Calvin, Bucer was no role model; he was ponderous and verbose, unable generally to match his material to a subject appropriately. On the other hand, Calvin's writing excelled in clarity, logicality and brevity.

At Strasbourg, besides being paid a florin a week for teaching the New Testament in a newly-founded High School, Calvin was busy with his books. First in importance was a second Latin edition of the *Institutes*, published in 1539 (later published in French in 1542). In the same year, Calvin's first commentary appeared—on the *Epistle to the Romans*. Besides showing the author's solidarity with Martin Luther over the doctrine of justification by faith in Christ alone, this work demonstrated at once that he was—and remains to this day—a 'prince of exegetes.' Serving to illustrate Calvin's spiritual warmth and musical interest, he also published his first psalter *Aulcuns pseaulmes et cantiques mys en chant* (1539). A highly significant development in Reformed worship, the collection contained eighteen psalms and three canticles—the song of Simeon, the Ten Commandments and the Apostles' Creed. Psalm 36 is set to the magnificent tune by Matthaus Greiter, used later for Psalm 68, the Huguenot 'battle hymn.' Seven of these psalms were versified by Calvin himself. Typical of his humility, he later withdrew them in favour of superior versions by Marot and Beza. Calvin also wrote an important reply to Cardinal Sadolet who, in the absence of the reformer, tried to seduce the people of Geneva back to the Roman fold. Less concerned with his own hurts than the cause of God's truth, Calvin's banishment did not stop him producing—in the space of only six days—a document vital for the preservation and development of the Genevan reformation. Denying the charge of novelty, Calvin explained that he was concerned with reforming the church rather than starting something new, arguing that the reformers had antiquity on their side *vis-à-vis* the claims of Rome.

Marriage

Calvin's days in Strasbourg were nothing if not hectic. Proof reading, sermon preparation, letter writing, receiving visitors and settling controversies were all part of his regular routine. With regard to the last, he was particularly successful in persuading Anabaptists to renounce their objections to infant baptism. Among the many asking

Calvin to baptise their children was Jean Stordeur of Liège and his wife Idelette de Bure, who was later to become Mme Calvin. While Calvin was strongly opposed to obligatory celibacy, he seemed devoid of romantic inclinations. Yet, showing signs of stress and irritability, Calvin was urged by Bucer and others to get married. On more than one occasion he was told, "You need a wife, Calvin." The Lord's provision for him—after three 'recommendations' were considered—was to be Idelette de Bure, whose husband died of the plague in the spring of 1540. She was attractive and cultured, a woman of good character and quiet strength. She was a perfect match for the brilliant yet temperamental reformer.

So, in August, John and Idelette were married, the ceremony being performed by Farel. Even though Calvin had said 'I am none of those insane lovers ... smitten at first sight with a fine figure', there's no denying that the marriage was happy in every respect. This is evident in Calvin's 'thank you' letter to Farel, despite the fact that the newly-weds became ill shortly after the wedding: "As if it had been so ordered, that our wedlock might not be overjoyous, the Lord thus thwarted our joy by moderating it." During a lengthy period involving unavoidable attendance at several 'ecumenical' discussions between Roman Catholics and Protestants (at the instigation of the Emperor Charles V), Calvin's fondness and concern for Idelette was obvious. Hearing that a plague was raging at Strasbourg, he wrote anxiously, "Day and night my wife has been constantly in my thoughts." However, she (with her two children by her previous marriage) was to survive, ready to accompany her husband on the next stage of his extraordinary career.

Recalled to Geneva

Towards the end of 1540, with the city bordering on anarchy, an official delegation from Geneva pleaded with Calvin to return to the city. Naturally he was reluctant even to consider the idea, not least that he now had a wife and family to care for. Clearly the pain of banishment still lingered. What? Geneva, again? "I should prefer a hundred other deaths rather than this cross on which I should have to die a thousand times a day," he protested. However, undeterred, Farel's importunities proved irresistible. Laying aside every other consideration but the cause of Christ, Calvin eventually wrote to Farel on 24 October 1540, "I offer my heart to God as a sacrifice." Still wrestling with anxious foreboding, attendance at the Colloquies of Worms (November 1540) and Ratisbon (April 1541) gave him good excuses to delay any move. Yet, finally yielding himself to the constraints of divine providence, Calvin entered Geneva for the second time on 13 September 1541.

Before we briefly survey Calvin's remaining twenty-three years in Geneva, a completion of the 'family' picture is appropriate, if only to dispel popular allegations about his 'lack of humanity.' Indeed, Calvin's religion did not make him a heartless Huguenot (or a pitiless Puritan) as too many ignorant critics would have us believe. First, we should remember that he was invited back to Geneva as the city's religious leader. His principles had not changed since his banishment three years earlier. Indeed, the people had changed in their estimate of him. In fact, gifts were showered upon him, including a new robe of black velvet trimmed with fur. The new family house at 11 Rue de Chanoines (now Rue Jean-Calvin), a narrow street near the cathedral of St. Pierre, was an improvement on the crowded boarding house at Strasbourg. There was a good-size garden overlooking Lake Leman. Then, to confirm the city's goodwill to God's servant, the Council sent a herald with a two-horse carriage to bring Idelette, the children and all the family furniture from Strasbourg to their new home. Idelette obviously enjoyed the new garden. Besides vegetables, she also planted herbs and sweet-scented flowers. When her husband had visitors, Calvin proudly showed off his wife's cultivations.

For all their married joy, the Calvins had sadness. The following summer (1542), Idelette had a premature son. Little Jacques lived only two weeks. Calvin responded with sad resignation sweetened with faith: "The Lord has certainly inflicted a bitter wound in the death of our infant son. But He is Himself a father and knows what is good for His children." Three years later, a daughter died at birth. After another two years (1547), a third child died after a premature birth. Not without enemies still in Geneva (and some insulted the reformer by naming their dogs after him), the Calvins were told that God was punishing them in their childlessness. Calvin's faith and courage rose in response: "My sons are to be found all over the world." Noted earlier (and worthy of repetition here), these bold words had a prophetic ring about them, as subsequent Huguenot history (not to forget the rest of Europe and beyond) was gloriously to demonstrate. Yet the suffering was not over. Sadness and gossip took their toll as Idelette's health began to deteriorate.

Calvin bereaved

After nine years of marriage, during which Idelette had provided her husband with godly emotional solace, she died, probably of tuberculosis. As she lay dying, her fervent testimony shows that her end was nothing if not triumphant: "O glorious resurrection! O God of Abraham and of all our fathers, the believers of all ages have trusted in Thee and none of them have hoped in vain. And now I fix my hope on Thee." Comforted by Idelette's serene passing, Calvin still felt devastated. Writing to Pierre Viret, we see Calvin at his most personal: "You know how tender, or rather, soft my heart is. If I did not have strong self-control I would not have been able to stand it this long. My grief is very heavy. My best life's companion has been taken from me. Whenever I faced serious difficulties she was ever ready to share with me, not only banishment and poverty, but even death itself." To Farel he wrote: "I do what I can to keep myself from being overwhelmed with grief. My friends also leave nothing undone that may bring relief to my mental suffering. ... May the Lord Jesus ... support me under this heavy affliction." Such was the grief of a man who had obviously known human love at its highest and deepest. Calvin never remarried. With his 'heart offered to his heavenly Father as a sacrifice', he thereafter bravely pursued a solitary life in the cause of Christ, fathering, guiding and comforting spiritual children by his astonishing ministry. This ministry continued after his death through anointed publications which continue to enrich his readers to the present day.

The Genevan ministry resumed

Having arrived from Strasbourg, almost as if nothing had happened between banishment and recall, Calvin went up into the pulpit of St. Pierre on the following Lord's Day and simply resumed his ministry where he had left off. That sermon was the overture to an astonishing output which makes up the bulk of the *Corpus Reformatorum*. It also reminds us that, when all is considered, the author of the *Institutes* was primarily and pre-eminently a 'preacher of the Word.' At first it seems he preached twice on Sunday and once on Monday, Wednesday and Friday, until in 1542—by popular demand—he was urged to preach more regularly. He did so for about seven years, but his health broke down around the time of his wife's death. In 1549, Denis Raguenier was employed as scribe to record Calvin's sermons, and from that year on we have remarkable manuscript material of all the scriptural expositions he delivered. It was now his usual practice to preach every week-day on alternate weeks, and three times on a Sunday, that is, ten times in every fourteen day period. During the week he preached on the Old Testament and on the New Testament on Sundays, sometimes expounding Psalms on a Sunday afternoon. The statistics reveal the scale of his dedication. On Sundays he preached 189 sermons from the Acts of the Apostles between 1549 and 1554; 384 (at least) sermons on the Pauline Epistles from 1554 to 1558, and 65 sermons on the Gospels from 1559 to 1564. During the week he preached a series on Jeremiah and Lamentations until 1550; the Minor Prophets and Daniel, 1550 to 1552; 174 sermons on Ezekiel 1552 to 1554; 159 on Job 1554 to 1555; 200 on Deuteronomy 1555 to 1556; 342 on Isaiah 1556 to 1559; 123 on Genesis 1559 to 1561; some on Judges in the same year; 107 on 1 Samuel and 87 on 2 Samuel 1561 to 1563; and on Kings in 1563 to 1564. Besides this phenomenal pulpit labour, we must also remember the commentaries which he wrote, not to forget the lectures he gave in the Geneva Academy! The only books of Scripture Calvin failed to expound were the Song of Solomon and Revelation, the second of which he apparently claimed not fully to understand. That said, his preaching and writing programme is simply breathtaking!

Calvin was clearly driven by a high purpose, to build up the Church of Christ and promote the spiritual maturity of his enthusiastic hearers. As the Reformation's Paul, Calvin strove to preach 'the whole counsel of God' (*Acts 20:27*). Who else, in the history of the Church, can match him in emulating the apostle's example?

Of all the reformers, who was clearer or more vigorous in asserting the claims of Christ than John Calvin? Since the issues he addressed so effectively are still with us, his contribution has lost none of its relevance, as two sermon examples demonstrate:

> And seeing that the Son of God is come, is it reasonable that men should put forth their own dreams and traditions, and that Jesus Christ should hold His peace? But the Popish religion tends to none other end, than to put Jesus Christ to silence. The Pope boasts himself to be His vicar. But however the case stands, he makes laws at his own pleasure: he makes new articles of faith: to be short, the [true] Gospel is but an aside, if we believe the Pope: and the traditions that he has devised are the full perfection of all. For behold, they have not been ashamed to say, that the things which the Popes and their councils have decreed, and all their rituals, filth and pelting trash, (which yet notwithstanding are but devilish abominations to pervert the service of God) are the things which the Apostles could not bear, when Jesus Christ said to them, "I still have many things to say to you, but you cannot bear them now" (*Jn. 16:12*). And what things be they? O they be the high mysteries which the Pope devised about the Gospel [the mass, cult of Mary, purgatory, etc]. Like as Muhammad says that his *Qur'an* is the sovereign wisdom: so says the Pope of his own decrees: For they be the two horns of Antichrist. Since it is so, do we not see that we cannot in anywise cleave to the Pope but by renouncing Jesus Christ. Then let us bear well in mind, that seeing it is God's will to exalt His only Son after that fashion: surely He will have us to look unto Him, and that all doctrine be referred unto Him, and do concern Him. So we must conclude that all who will speak in the Church, must utter nothing but that which they have learned in the school of this great Schoolmaster (*Sermon on Deuteronomy 18:9–15*).

Those, therefore, who fully support the Pope wish to keep the filthy abominations that they have always practised right to the end. However, there are many others who wish to see a reformation take place to the end that they might mix together in one the Pope, Muhammad and Jesus Christ, so that we can no longer discern between them! It makes no difference to them, provided they can bring the whole world together in harmony. They do not have a scrap of reverence for God. This explains why everything is so muddled and confused in our day, hence the abomination known as liberalism has arisen. Because they could not find it in their hearts to agree with Popery in every point, they thought it would be better if they were to reach a compromise between all the extremes (*Sermon on Galatians 2:3–5*).

There are many indications that Calvin's extraordinary ministry was abundantly blest of God in the hearts of his ever-eager hearers. As proof of the constant appetite for his preaching and books, we get a glimpse of the preacher himself from one reader, Jean de l'Espine. Despite the lofty and solemn themes of his faithful ministry, the wonderful loving-kindness of God always shone through. Calvin was no 'heavy' and austere presenter of God's truth: 'Although we cannot hear your sweet voice and see your happy face, we are able to enjoy reading your books.' This description of the reformer indicates a grossly neglected side of his personality—his genuine 'human touch.' His theological preoccupations did not preclude humanitarian concern. On the contrary, they inspired practical love of one's neighbour. Thus Calvin involved himself in the problems of unemployment, the city's sewage system and plans to improve heating.

While his intense dedication to his calling have created a rather dour impression, Calvin could be relaxed and even playful. Alexander Morus, a seventeenth-century professor in the Genevan Academy, states that 'with a great zeal and vehemence, there was combined a cheerful, even gay disposition' in John Calvin. Beza (who knew Calvin at close quarters) said similarly that 'with regard to his manners, although nature had formed him for gravity, yet, in the common intercourse of life, there was no man who was more pleasant.' Morus continues: 'However little we may know of his agreeable conversation, and gentle, familiar bearing, we know this, on the report of persons worthy of credit, that he made no difficulty of amusing himself at a game with messieurs our magistrates; but it was the innocent game called *la clef*, the aim of which consists in pushing a certain number of keys as near as possible from one end to the other of a long table.' Another example of his kind disposition concerns Calvin's dealings with young people. When sending a letter to Pierre Viret by one of two students, he noticed that the other looked crest-fallen at not being the messenger. Calvin quickly penned a new letter for the other lad to take, asking Viret to pretend to treat it as an important communication!

Commentaries, Institutes and correspondence

Besides his preaching, Calvin wrote and published numerous books. In his commentaries (from Romans, 1540 to Joshua, 1564), when specific passages required doctrinal enlargement, Calvin often refers the reader to his *Institutes*. His *magnum opus*—'a work of great toil'—was constantly revised by its author, passing through several editions until the final one of 1559. Translated into several European languages, it became the 'text book' of the Reformed Faith wherever Calvin's literary influence spread. While the immortal *Institutes*—loved and lamented by friend and foe respectively—requires little advertisement here, less is popularly known about his voluminous correspondence. Writing from 11 Rue de Chanoines to Christians high and low, to European Heads of State as well as church leaders, his home may be regarded as the Genevan 'Foreign Office'! Always the pastor, Calvin expressed warm concern for other pastors, grieving parents, backsliders and Protestants awaiting martyrdom. Calvin's deep affection is undisguised in a letter regarding Theodore Beza's illness of 1551:

> I was seized with fresh alarm, and, at the same time, weighed down with a load of grief. For I was informed, the day before, that he had been seized with the plague. I was therefore not only troubled about the danger he was in, but from my very great affection for him I felt almost over-powered, as if I was already lamenting his death; although, indeed, this grief did not rise so much from private regard, as from my public anxiety for the prosperity of the Church. Indeed, I were destitute of human feeling, did I not return the affection of one who loves me with more than a brother's love, and reveres me like a very father.

His letters to the 'five students of Lausanne', martyred in Lyons in

1553, are touching examples of his faithful and tender involvement
with those willing to suffer for the cause of Christ in France. As
was generally the case, Calvin's concern for God's kingdom takes
precedence over simply human considerations (without devaluing
the latter in any degree). Learning of the sufferings of these young
heroes of Christ, the reformer wrote:

> Now, although these tidings have proved sorrowful to the flesh,
> even in consequence of the love we justly bear you in God, as we are
> bound to do, yet we submit ourselves to the will of this kind Father
> and sovereign Lord, and not only consider His way of disposing of
> us just and reasonable, but also accept it with a gentle and loving
> heart as altogether right and profitable for our salvation, …

Towards the end of his life, this same concern is seen in letters
to Huguenot leaders like Gaspar de Coligny. England too had a
significant share in his epistolary attention. Writing to the Duke of
Somerset in the reign of King Edward VI (1547–53), Calvin urged
further reform, especially regarding preaching. Little impressed
by the English *Book of Common Prayer*, he stressed the need for
'good trumpets.' Somewhat disappointed at the slow progress of
reformation in England, Calvin urged Archbishop Thomas Cranmer
to be more thorough and decisive. In warm response to Cranmer's
proposal for a General Synod of the Reformed Churches, Calvin
the ardent ecumenist declared that he 'would not grudge to cross
even ten seas, if need were, on account of it.' Another change of
monarch in England ensured that such an event would not occur.
Lamenting the setbacks and sufferings of Mary Tudor's reactionary
reign (1553–58), Calvin later exhorted Protestant Elizabeth to
promote spiritual rather than secular authority in the Church of
England. Judging by his correspondence with Edmund Grindall,
Bishop of London, Calvin gave impetus to the growth of Puritanism
in the semi-reformed Anglican church.

III

Order, Worship and Liturgy

As we have seen, Calvin argued for Presbyterian government in the Church. Compared with the retention of episcopacy in the Church of England, Calvin's case is thoroughly rooted in Scripture, as his comment on Acts 20:28 makes clear:

> About the word *bishops* we must briefly note that Paul calls all the Ephesian presbyters this, without distinction. From that we gather that, according to the usage of Scripture, bishops do not differ from presbyters in any way. But through vice and corruption it came about that those who held the leading place in individual cities, began to be called 'bishops'. I say 'vice', not because it is a bad thing for any one man to be prominent in [an eldership], but because it is an intolerable presumption, when men twist the words of Scripture to their own customs, and do not hesitate to change the language of the Holy Spirit.

Unlike the ambiguous retention of 'priest' in the Anglican *Book of Common Prayer*, Calvin demonstrated that Christian ministry is 'prophetic' rather than 'priestly'. Indeed, Calvin and the French Reformed churches were opposed to sacrificing priests in favour of preaching pastors. The advocates of a spurious theory of apostolic succession claimed to ensure a line of sacrificing priests, the diocesan bishop being 'the symbol of priestcraft'. These concerns are not confined to the time of the Reformation. The reformed Anglican understanding of the Gospel continues to be hampered by an ambiguous and unscriptural term. This is not to call in question the entirely separate and valid issue of the priesthood of all believers. Notwithstanding all the rationalizing endeavours of the conservative evangelical Anglican tradition, none can doubt that the retention of 'priest' has ensured that recent and ongoing controversy with Anglo-Catholics over the unscriptural ordination of women to the priesthood has hinged on medieval theories of priesthood.

This 'Anglican ambiguity' only clouds the gospel as debates on the issue have proved. For instance, the question 'can a woman represent Christ at the altar?' is a non-starter. And why? The only altar recognised by God is the cross on Calvary's hill; the only atoning

sacrifice recognised by God is that once-for-all offering of Christ;
and the only priesthood recognised by God is that of His only-
begotten Son. This, quite simply, is the message of the Epistle to
the Hebrews, as Calvin was quick to point out. For these reasons,
Calvin's view of order and ministry—Reformed *ecclesiology*—was a
necessary expression of Reformed *soteriology*. The Reformed churches
of Geneva, France, the Netherlands, Scotland and elsewhere believed
that Christ's sacrifice for sin is remembered not repeated, on a table,
not an altar; His real presence is spiritual, not physical, in the hearts of
His people and not in the bread and wine. Hence Christian ministers
are pastors, not priests, called to honour Christ's unique priesthood,
not to set up a hierarchy.

While Calvin rejected the Roman mass and the false theory
of baptismal regeneration, he did not, as we have noted, reject
infant baptism. His baptismal teaching was rooted in the theology
of the covenant. Thus as Jewish parents honoured God's promises
to their children in observing circumcision, so Christian parents
do likewise in the sacrament of baptism. In Calvin's view of the
transition from the Old Testament to the New, the covenant of
grace continued even though the covenant sign changed. This
teaching is comprehensively set out in the *Institutes* and in the
reformer's Bible commentaries.

The continuity from the Old testament to the New is also
seen in Calvin's advocacy of psalm singing. The Genevan *Psalter*,
consisting of Marot's and Beza's paraphrases—employing varied
metres and set to the majestic and glorious tunes of Greiter and
Bourgeois—was vitally important in Calvin's reform of worship.
Even the music was to be appropriately composed. The reformer
wrote that 'Whatever people may enjoy at home, the music of
worship in the presence of God and the angels must not be light
and frothy, but must have weight and majesty'. Here then are the
psalms which inspired the heroic Huguenots in their sufferings
for Christ. There was nothing drab about Reformed worship at
the beginning, judging by the experience of a student passing
through Strasbourg in 1545 where, as we noted earlier, Calvin
had published his first Psalter just six years before:

> You would never believe what a happy thing it is and what peace of conscience one experiences in being where the Word of God is purely proclaimed and the sacraments purely administered. Also when one hears the fine Psalms sung and the marvellous works of the Lord... At the beginning when I heard the singing I could scarcely keep myself from weeping with joy. You would not hear one voice drowning another. Everybody holds a book of music in his hand. Every man and woman alike praises the Lord.

Calvin was not exclusively committed to the Old Testament Psalms, since the Genevan *Psalter* included metrical versions of the Lord's Prayer, the Ten Commandments, the Song of Simeon and the Apostles' Creed. As we have seen, civil interference in Geneva frustrated Calvin's desires for weekly communion, and there is evidence that he preferred the worship of Strasbourg to that of Geneva, where hymns were sung as well as psalms. In 1545 Calvin prepared a third edition of his liturgy *La Forme des Prières* for the use of his former congregation in Strasbourg. His outline of the ideal Sunday morning service hardly suggests exclusive psalmody; it also says something about the warmth and breadth of Calvin's 'Calvinism'—a subject we are shortly to consider: 'We begin with the confession of our sins, adding readings from the Law and the Gospel (that is, sentences of remission) ... and after we are assured that as Jesus Christ has righteousness and life in Himself, and that He lives for the sake of the Father, so we are justified in Jesus Christ and live in a new life by the same Jesus Christ ... we continue with psalms, hymns of praise, the reading of the Gospel ... and ... quickened and stirred by the reading and preaching of the Gospel, and the confession of our faith (that is, Apostles' Creed) ... it follows that we must pray for the salvation of all men for the life of Christ should be greatly enkindled within us. Now the life of Christ consists in this, namely, to seek and save that which is lost...'

The Servetus affair

Beside his efforts to succour the young martyrs of Lyons, Calvin had another less noble preoccupation in 1553. Having previously noted Calvin's abortive attempt to reclaim Michael Servetus from his anti-Trinitarianism in Paris, the Spaniard came to Geneva and boldly challenged the author of the *Institutes* with his own *Christianismi Restitutio* (1553). Without staying with the details of this tragic episode, Calvin's part in the eventual trial, condemnation and execution of Servetus has sadly stained his memory and ruined his reputation ever since in the eyes of many. Indeed, in no way can the heretic's treatment be justified. Calvin was simply wrong to believe that the death penalty was to be administered to heretics (a defective view that was later sanctioned in Article 39 of the Huguenot Confession, the *Confessio Fidei Gallicana* (1559). However, while he did not deny that such punishment was valid 'against the first as well as against the second table of the Commandments of God,' Calvin—despite the bitterness of Servetus' attack on him— did his utmost to mitigate the punishment, to replace burning with a less inhumane method. A proper assessment of the tragedy was not helped by Voltaire's malicious 18th century attack on the 'dictator' of Geneva. The simple fact is that, contrary to the personal malice of Voltaire, the heretic was condemned by the Magistrates of Geneva, with the concurrence of the Swiss cities of Berne, Basle, Zurich and Schaffhausen. Not to forget that, had the Roman Catholics secured the heretic's arrest they would have had no qualms about his execution, the whole episode was but one error of the age. Indeed, it took longer for the Reformed churches to jettison from their thinking the barbarity they had inherited from Rome. The idea that Calvin relished the agonies of the burning heretic is as false as the charge that he was a 'dictator,' with all the diabolical overtones and connotations of the Fascist and Nazi regimes of the twentieth century. In fact, Calvin was distressed by the whole episode and wished to resign.

Two more points are to be considered. *First*, in the spirit of Calvin's distress, an expiatory monument was erected in Geneva in 1903 by the Reformed Churches of Geneva and France. A big question is: did the Roman Catholics of Europe do anything similar for the thousands of Protestant martyrs they incinerated and destroyed? *Second*, without seeking entirely to absolve Calvin for his part, it is true to say he was less guilty than others. Also, it is impossible for us to appreciate the seriousness of the situation in an age which is so indifferent to Christian truth and the necessity of church discipline. Calvin was right to insist on Trinitarian orthodoxy and the deity of Christ, without which the entire Reformation movement would have floundered and sunk as it did in Socinian Poland. Unlike all religious groups who persist in denying the deity and uniqueness of our Lord Jesus Christ, at least there is some hope for Michael Servetus. Indeed, is there not evidence that Calvin's efforts to convince his antagonist of his unbelief were not in vain? The possibly-penitent heretic died with the prayer, "Eternal Son of God, have pity on me."

Calvin and predestination

Clearly then, it is impossible to isolate the Servetus affair from the recovery of authentic Christian truth which was the Protestant Reformation. That said, it is no part of the Reformed legacy to deny that there were some mistakes in that recovery. However, the recovery of the doctrine of salvation by grace alone without the merit of works—with its corollary of divine predestination—was no mistake. Besides his treatment of the subject of predestination in successive editions of the *Institutes*, the issue received Calvin's special attention in two other major publications. Just as Luther defended the sovereignty of God in his reply to Erasmus' views on free will in 1525, so Calvin engaged with Albert Pighius of Kampen on the subject in 1543. Then, in 1551, controversy over predestination with Jérôme Bolsec in Geneva contributed to a further treatise against Pighius from Calvin, *Concerning the Eternal Predestination of God* (1552).

For all the animosity aroused against Calvin on account of predestination, the hostility has its roots in the Pelagianised 'man-centred' thinking of scholars like Erasmus and Pighius, the result of several centuries of doctrinal decay within the medieval church. Apart from the fact that Calvin's ultimate defence is the apostolic teaching of his 'mentor' Paul (who arguably obtained it from Christ his Lord), he had a precedent in 'link man' Augustine of Hippo (354–430) whose last treatise *Concerning the Predestination of the Saints* (429 AD) helped earn him the title 'Doctor of Grace.' Add to this that all the major churches of the Reformation—including the Church of England—affirmed predestination in their confessions, it becomes utterly absurd to 'blame' Calvin for teaching predestination (even if it's the 'double' nature that is most objected to). It is also equally incorrect to highlight predestination as the major feature of Calvinism, a caricature probably due to the overly-systematic approach of Calvin's successor Theodore Beza. This sad rationalising tendency, exacerbated by later scholastic theological developments, led to emphases and deductions not to be charged upon Calvin himself, e.g. the doctrine of 'limited atonement.'

A proper understanding of Calvin's teaching demands the following considerations:

1. Notwithstanding his specialist treatments of the subject, it is noteworthy that the doctrine of predestination has a lower profile in Calvin's overall thought than it does in later Calvinist theology of the Bezan/*Westminster Confession* type. Just as Paul—in the context of assurance—delays discussion of the subject until chapters 8 and 9 of his *Epistle to the Romans*, it appears for the same reason—late in Book III of Calvin's *Institutes*, where, like Paul, the author provides the ultimate reason (as a concomitant to unbelief) why some are saved and others are lost.

2. While seeking to be a faithful servant of the Word of God, Calvin still acknowledges the decree of reprobation to be 'dreadful' (*Inst.* 3:23:7). Clearly taking no improper delight in teaching it, his unequivocal affirmation of it was blended with humility and caution. He plainly taught—while affirming an ultimate agnosticism over the advent of sin—that while God providentially arranges all the factors behind human choices—***without being the author of sin***, the 'cause and matter' of reprobation is foreknown human guilt rather than a naked supralapsarian decree (see *Inst.* 3:23:7–9).

3. For all that he has been charged with 'double predestination', Calvin requires a more nuanced interpretation. He is clear

that, since 'amazing' *external* grace is the cause of undeserved salvation (the elect being no more worthy than others), *internal* sin is the cause of deserved damnation (see *Inst.* 3:23:11). Hence the twin decrees of salvation and damnation are not strictly 'parallel.' Calvin has arguably been misrepresented in other respects too. Contrary to later ill-informed Arminian and *ultra*-Calvinist discussion, Calvin even denied that the human will—man being a voluntary slave—is divinely coerced. He seems also quite happy to admit the term 'free will,' provided it is carefully defined (see *Inst.* 2:2:7–8). Such is Calvin's amazing biblical balance!

4. In dealing with the issues pastorally, Calvin warned that 'whoever is not satisfied with Christ but inquires curiously about eternal predestination desires, as far as lies in him, to be saved contrary to God's purpose. The election of God in itself is hidden and secret. ... Therefore, they are mad who seek their own or others' salvation in the labyrinth of predestination; for if God has elected us to the end that we may believe, take away faith and election will be imperfect' (*Comm.* Jn. 6:40). Thus 'knowledge of salvation is not to be demanded by us out of the secret counsel of God. Life is set before us in Christ, who not only makes Himself known in the Gospel but also presents Himself to be enjoyed. Let the eye of faith look fixedly in this mirror, and not try to penetrate where access is not open' (*The Eternal Predestination of God*).

A closely related and relevant issue concerns the 'tension' between God's 'hidden' absolute *purposes* and his 'revealed' conditional *promises*. Rooted in his dualistic conception of the divine will (see *Deut. 29:29*), Calvin taught that Christ was offered as the Redeemer of the whole world according to God's 'revealed' conditional will albeit only received by elected believers according to God's 'hidden' absolute will. Notwithstanding the rationally-challenging paradox involved, Calvin—like Paul—maintained the doctrines of universal atonement and divine election side by side. Faced by clear biblical evidence for both, he refused to tamper with the scriptural texts. Logic was not allowed to dictate one emphasis at the expense of the other. In this regard, a single specimen from his *Eternal Predestination* (IX. 5) illustrates Calvin's position perfectly:

> It is incontestable that Christ came for the expiation of the sins of the whole world. But the solution lies close at hand, that whosoever believes in Him should not perish but should have eternal life (*Jn. 3:15*). … Hence, we conclude that, though reconciliation is offered to all through Him, yet the benefit is peculiar to the elect, that they may be gathered into the society of life. However, while I say it is offered to all, I do not mean that this embassy, by which on Paul's testimony (*2 Cor. 5:18*) God reconciles the world to Himself, reaches to all, but that it is not sealed indiscriminately on the hearts of all to whom it comes so as to be effectual.

This is 'authentic Calvinism'! Furthermore, a correct grasp of Calvin's views perfectly answers two criticisms of Calvinism: *first,* that it is impossible to be compassionately evangelistic if one is a 'Calvinist'; and *second,* that Calvin fathered a theology destitute of a missionary dimension. Whatever became sadly true of derivatives of Calvinism initiated by Beza (and developed by the English divines John Owen and John Gill), three quotations from Calvin refute both charges:

> Christ brought life because the heavenly Father does not wish the human race that He loves to perish. … For although there is nothing in the world deserving of God's favour, He nevertheless shows He is favourable to the whole world when He calls all without exception to the faith of Christ, which is indeed an entry into life (*Comm. Jn. 3:16*).
>
> And indeed, our Lord Jesus was offered to all the world. For it is not speaking of three or four when it says: 'God so loved the world, that He spared not His only Son.' But yet we must notice what the Evangelist adds in this passage: 'That whosoever believes in Him shall not perish but obtain eternal life.' Our Lord Jesus suffered for all and there is neither great nor small who is not inexcusable today, for we can obtain salvation in Him. Unbelievers who turn away from Him and who deprive themselves of Him by their malice are today doubly culpable. For how will they excuse their ingratitude in not receiving the blessing in which they could share by faith? And let us realize that if we come flocking to our Lord Jesus Christ, we shall not hinder one another and prevent Him being sufficient for each of us…Let us not fear to come to Him in great numbers, and each one of us bring his neighbours, seeing that He is sufficient to save us all (*Sermons on Isaiah 53*).

> Let us fall down before the face of our good God...that it may please Him to grant His grace, not only to us, but also to all people and nations of the earth, bringing back all poor ignorant souls from the miserable bondage of error and darkness, to the right way of salvation... (*Calvin's usual end of sermon prayer*).

There is absolutely no doubt (as I have argued extensively elsewhere) that Calvin's God-glorifying agenda entailed and inspired *universal* evangelistic endeavour (see *Comms.* Jn. 12:47; Mk. 16:16). Shunning a preoccupation with predestination (yet humbly acknowledging its profound reality), his priority was to urge people to look to Christ in whom grace is universally available. From the *Romans* commentary of 1540 to his *Last Will* of 1564, it is easy to demonstrate that this was Calvin's consistent concern. Indeed (as he repeatedly maintained), while the outcome of gospel endeavour is ultimately in God's hands, the church's function in the world is to be directed by God's universal gracious will. In which case, the challenge of Calvin's stance is not how to resolve the soteriological antinomy at the heart of his theology (in either a Bezan or an Arminian direction) but to adopt his guiding principle: 'Our true wisdom is to embrace with meek docility, and without reservation, whatever the Holy Scriptures have delivered' (*Inst.* 1:18:4). These observations also have significance for the next chapter, in which we will consider—among other things—the claims of Calvin's fellow-countryman Moïse Amyraut (1596–1664) to perpetuate the reformer's 'authentic Calvinism.'

IV

The Triumph of the Truth

Calvin's years in Geneva involved constant struggle for the Reformed Faith. To conflicts over major theological issues was added opposition to his personal influence. As we have seen, for all his authority and eminence, this so-called dictator failed to achieve all his reformation goals. Besides personal insults in the streets, others would fire guns outside his door, almost frightening the 'timid and fearful' man out of his wits. Sometimes while he was preaching, boys caused annoying distractions by throwing stones at the windows of St. Pierre. However, under the blessing of God, by the mid-1550s Calvin's perseverance was being rewarded. Concerned to uphold the right of the Consistory (the board of elders) to discipline and excommunicate loose-living hypocrites, Calvin won his battle over Philibert Berthelier, one of Geneva's most notorious 'libertines.' Expecting to resign his ministry once again over this crisis, Calvin was eventually backed by the city Council which had earlier looked with sympathy on Berthelier's request to attend the Lord's Supper. Besides increasing support within the city councils, more citizens were accepting the teachings and example of the reformer and his brethren, popular support being augmented by the many French Protestant refugees flocking to Geneva. Indeed, men destined for fame in their own lands came under Calvin's influence. Guido de Brès from the Netherlands, author of the *Belgic Confession* (1561) sat at the reformer's feet in 1556. That same year, the well-known Scottish reformer John Knox declared to a friend that 'I have no fear at all of saying that Geneva is the most perfect school of Christ that has ever been on the earth since the time of the apostles. Elsewhere, I grant, Christ is preached in all truth, but I know no town in which religion and morals are so thoroughly reformed.' Truly, the city's motto 'Post tenebras lux' was highly appropriate. After centuries of darkness, a new dawn had come, for Geneva, France, Europe and the world!

The Genevan Academy

For three reasons, the year 1559 was a highpoint for Calvin. Besides becoming a citizen of Geneva, the final edition of his monumental *Institutes* was published. Of equally-far reaching importance that year was the foundation of the Academy on 15 June 1559. A dispute between the faculty of Lausanne and the Bernese government over the rights of excommunication (the battle Calvin also had to fight), brought Theodore Beza, Pierre Viret and three other professors to Geneva. This brilliant team of teachers was to make the Genevan Academy famous throughout Europe. Besides becoming Calvin's right-hand man, Beza was appointed both Professor of

Greek and the first Rector. As if drawn by the magnet of truth, students flocked to Geneva from all parts. It thus became the intellectual centre of the French-speaking Reformation. Here pastors were trained for service in France where churches were settled and growing with amazing rapidity. In this year when the first National Synod of the French Reformed churches was held in Paris, Calvin's pastoral and missionary zeal inspired the lofty aims of this Christian college: 'Send us wood and we will send you back arrows.' Between 1555 and 1562, eighty-eight men were sent out according to the *Register of the Company of the Pastors*. While some names were not recorded for security reasons, a total of one hundred and forty-two were sent out in one peak year. The Rector's book of student names lists notable men who later made their mark in the service of Christ. One is Kaspar Olevianus of the German Reformed Church, co-author (with Zacharias Ursinus, who also visited Geneva) of the famous *Heidelberg Catechism* (1563). Another is Thomas Bodley from England, whose son founded the Bodleian Library at Oxford.

Journey's end

Considering all his labours and conflicts, it is inconceivable that Calvin would live long. Never robust in health, a serious fever he had suffered during 1558–9 was followed by lung problems after overstraining his voice in preaching. Violent coughing at home ruptured a blood-vessel in his lungs accompanied by bad haemorrhaging. From this time, the reformer's health deteriorated. Though suffering also from kidney stones and piles, and with the onset of tuberculosis, Calvin continued working with amazing fortitude. Concern for the persecuted infant Reformed churches of France added to his burdens. When attempts were made to promote national religious peace between Catholics and Protestants at the Colloquy of Poissy in September 1561, Calvin was too ill to attend. The courageous representation of Beza and his brethren eventually led to the document of religious toleration known as 'The Edict of January' (1562). However, with suspicion and intrigue continuing, a Huguenot worship service at Vassy in

Champagne was violently interrupted by troops of the Catholic
Duke of Guise on 1 March. Many worshippers being killed, this
appalling atrocity precipitated—after months of rising tensions
and failed political manoeuvring—the first battle of the French
wars of religion. Thus the Battle of Dreux was fought on 19
December, with disappointment for the Huguenot troops led by
the 'indomitable-in-defeat' Admiral Gaspar Coligny (with whom
Calvin had corresponded). In his biography of the reformer, Beza
records a fascinating occurrence on the day of the battle:

> On the 19th of December, which happened to be a Sabbath, Calvin
> was confined to bed with the gout. The north wind having continued
> to blow, with the greatest violence, for two successive days, Calvin,
> in the hearing of several persons, says, "I know not what the cause of
> it is, but during the night, I thought I heard martial music sounding
> aloud, and could not persuade myself that it was not really so. Let
> us pray, I beseech you; for some matter of great moment is going
> forward." It turned out that on that very day a fierce battle was fought
> at Dreux, though the news of it did not arrive for some days after.

By the beginning of 1563 Calvin 'was often carried to his duties
in a chair or on horseback.' He struggled on until February 1564,
spiritually undaunted yet a near-physical wreck, as his grateful
letter to the physicians of Montpellier—who had offered their
help—vividly illustrates. Clearly, any medical help was out of the
question by now. Realising that his end could not be far away,
his sixty-fifth and final lecture on Ezekiel given on Wednesday
afternoon, 2 February ended with an appropriate and moving prayer:

> Grant, Almighty God, since we have already entered in hope
> upon the threshold of our eternal inheritance, and know that there
> is a certain mansion for us in heaven after Christ has been received
> there, who is our head, and the first-fruits of our salvation: Grant, I
> say, that we may proceed more and more in the course of thy holy
> calling until at length we reach the goal, and so enjoy that eternal
> glory of which thou affordest us a taste in this world, by the same
> Christ our Lord.—Amen.

Calvin was present at worship in St Pierre for the last time on
Easter Day, 2 April. Suffering extreme exhaustion, 'he was carried
to the church in a chair', writes Beza, 'and was present during
the whole service. He received the Lord's Supper from my hand,

and sung the hymn along with the others, though with tremulous voice, yet with a look in which joy was not obscurely indicated on his dying countenance.'

Yet Calvin had a few more weeks to live. Not without a touch of humour, he wrote to his friend Henry Bullinger, the Zurich reformer on 6 April 1564 that 'all remedies have so far proved ineffectual. ... You will not be surprised then, if so many sufferings make me lazy. I can hardly be brought to take any food. The taste of the wine is bitter.' Beza remarks as follows:

> While oppressed with so many diseases, no man ever heard him utter a word unbecoming a man of firmness, far less unbecoming a Christian. Only raising his eyes towards heaven, he would say, "O Lord, how long;" for even when he was in health this was an expression which he often used in reference to the calamities of his brethren, which night and day affected him much more than his own sufferings. We advising and entreating him that while sick he should desist from all fatigue of dictating, or at least of writing,—"What," he would say, "would you have the Lord to find me idle?"

Calvin made his will on 25 April, the contents of which, however meagre his wealth, show a wisdom and generosity typical of the man. Above all, his faith shines in this document:

> I John Calvin, servant of the Word of God in the church of Geneva, weakened by many illnesses...thank God that he has not only shown mercy to me, his poor creature...and suffered me in all sins and weaknesses, but what is more than that, he has made me a partaker of his grace to serve him through my work...I confess to live and die in this faith which he has given me, inasmuch as I have no other hope or refuge than his predestination upon which my entire salvation is grounded. I embrace the grace which he has offered me in our Lord Jesus Christ, and accept the merits of his suffering and dying that through him all my sins are buried; and I humbly beg him to wash me and cleanse me with the blood of our great Redeemer, as it was shed for all poor sinners so that I, when I appear before his face, may bear his likeness.

He took his leave of the Little Council two days later, while on the following day, he bid farewell to the ministers and elders. Both occasions saw a profusion of tears, as God's loved and lamented servant set his face towards heaven. In a final and quite lengthy oration (including critical comments in the style of 'the accusative case'), Calvin revealed yet again, despite his weakening voice, the chief motivation of his ministry: 'I have always faithfully propounded what I esteemed to be for the glory of God.' Then, on 2 May, he expressed his last adieus to his old friend William Farel:

> Farewell, my most excellent and upright brother; and since it is the will of God that you should survive me in the world, live mindful of our intimacy, which, as it was useful to the church of God, so the fruits of it await us in heaven. I am unwilling that you should fatigue yourself for my sake. I draw my breath with difficulty, and every moment I am in expectation of breathing my last. It is enough that I live and die for Christ, who is to all his followers a gain both in life and death. Again I bid you and your brethren Farewell.

In spite of his age and infirmity, Farel did make an effort to visit Calvin, who died on 27 May 1564 aged 54 years and 10 months. Writing to a friend a few days later, Farel exclaimed, 'Oh, how happily he has run a noble race! May the Lord grant that we run like him, and according to the measure of grace that has been dealt out to us.' On learning of the reformer's passing, many desired to see the body. To avoid creating a saintly cult, he was buried two days later in the common cemetery known as the Plein Palais with 'no extraordinary pomp, and as he had commanded, without any grave stone', wrote Beza. And so Calvin's mortal remains await there still for the day of resurrection.

As we conclude this tribute to John Calvin, we quote a hymn attributed to him. Appearing originally in the *Strasbourg Psalter* (1545) and later quoted in a Genevan service book, these words (albeit an edited version of the original) convey perfectly the Christian spirit of its author. They sum up the legacy of the godly genius of Geneva, whose writings continued to inform and inspire the heroic testimony of the Huguenot people in the coming days and years:

I GREET Thee who my sure Redeemer art,
My only trust and Saviour of my heart,
Who pain didst undergo for my poor sake:
I pray Thee from our hearts all cares to take.

Thou art the King of mercy and of grace,
Reigning omnipotent in every place:
So come, O King, and our whole being sway;
Shine on us with the light of Thy pure day.

Thou art the Life, by which alone we live,
And all our substance and our strength receive;
O comfort us in death's approaching hour,
Strong-hearted then to face it by Thy power.

Thou hast the true and perfect gentleness,
No harshness hast Thou, and no bitterness;
O grant to us the grace we find in Thee,
That we may dwell in perfect unity.

Our hope is in no other save in Thee;
Our faith is built upon Thy promise free;
Come, give us peace, make us so strong and sure,
That we may conquerors be, and ills endure.

Further reading:

Amyraut, M., *Defensio doctrinae J. Calvini de absoluto reprobationis decreto* (Saumur: I. Desbordes, 1641).

— *Defense de la doctrine de Calvin* (Saumur: I. Desbordes, 1644).

Armstrong, B. G., *Calvinism and the Amyraut Heresy: Protestant Scholasticism and Humanism in Seventeenth-Century France* (Madison: University of Wisconsin Press, 1969).

Baird, H. M., *History of the Rise of the Huguenots* 2 vols., facs. (Stoke-on-Trent: Tentmaker Publications, 2007).

Benedict, P., *Christ's Churches Purely Reformed* (New Haven & London: Yale University Press, 2002)

— *The Faith and Fortunes of France's Huguenots* (Aldershot/Vermont: Ashgate, 2001).

Benoit, J. - D., *Calvin in His Letters* (Abingdon: Sutton Courtenay Press, 1986).

Benoist, E., *The History of the Edict of Nantes*, 2 vols (London: J. Dunton, 1694).

Bevan, F., *The Life of William Farel* (Addison, IL: Bible Truth Publishers,1975).

Bouwsma, W. J., *John Calvin: A Sixteenth-century Portrait* (New York: Oxford University Press, 1988).

Calvin, J. *Institutes of the Christian Religion*, ed. J. T. McNeill, tr. F. L. Battles, 2 vols. (Philadelphia: The Westminster Press, 1960).

— *Institutes of the Christian Religion*, tr. Henry Beveridge (London: J. Clarke, 1962).

— *Calvin's Commentaries*, D. W. Torrance, T. F. Torance (eds.), 12 vols. (Oliver & Boyd/St Andrew Press, 1959–).

— Bonnet, J., (ed), *Letters of John Calvin*, 4 vols (Edinburgh & New York: 1855–).

— *Letters of John Calvin, Selected from the Bonnet Edition* (Edinburgh: Banner of Truth Trust, 1980).

Clifford, A. C., *Atonement and Justification: English Evangelical Theology 1640–1790—An Evaluation* (Oxford: OUP, 1990, 2002).

— *Calvinus: Authentic Calvinism, A Clarification* (Norwich: Charenton Reformed Publishing, 1996; 2nd ed. 2007).

— *Amyraut Affirmed* (Norwich: Charenton Reformed Publishing, 2004).

— 'Bishop or Presbyter? French Reformed Ecclesiology in 1559', *The Evangelical Quarterly*, Vol. 67. 3 (July, 1995).

— Introduction to John Davenant, *A Dissertation on the Death of Christ* (Weston Rhyn: Quinta Press, 2006).

— (ed.), *Christ for the World: Affirming Amyraldianism* (Norwich: Charenton Reformed Publishing, 2007).

— 'John Calvin and the Confessio Fidei Gallicana', *The Evangelical Quarterly*, Vol. 58. 3 (July, 1986).

— 'The Westminster Directory of Public Worship (1645)', *The Reformation of Worship* (London: The Westminster Conference, 1989).

Cadier, J., *The Man God Mastered* (London: IVF, 1960).

Diefendorf, B. B., *Beneath the Cross: Catholics and Huguenots in Sixteenth-Century Paris* (Oxford: OUP, 1991).

Duke, A., Lewis, G., Pettegree, A., (eds), *Calvinism in Europe 1540–1610* (Manchester & New York: Manchester University Press, 1992).

Edwards, C. E., (ed.), *Devotions & Prayers of John Calvin* (Grand Rapids: Baker Book House, 1976).

Grant, A. J., *The Huguenots* (London: Thornton Butterworth, 1934).

Greef, W. de, *The Writings of John Calvin* (Grand Rapids: Baker Books/Apollos, 1993).

Greengrass, M., *The French Reformation* (Oxford: B. Blackwell, 1987).

Hugues, P. E., (ed.), *The Register of the Company of the Pastors of Geneva in the Time of Calvin* (Grand Rapids: Eerdmans, 1966).

Holt, Mack O., *Renaissance and Reformation France* (Oxford: Oxford University Press, 2002).

Martyn, W. C., *A History of the Huguenots* (New York: American Tract Society, 1866).

McGrath, A., *A Life of John Calvin* (Oxford: Basil Blackwell, 1990).

Parker, T. H. L., *John Calvin* (London: Lion Publishing, 1975).

Prestwich, M., (ed), *International Calvinism, 1541–1715* (Oxford: Oxford University Press, 1985).

Prothero, R. E., *The Psalms in Human Life* (London: T. Nelson, 1903).

Selderhuis, H., *John Calvin: A Pilgrim's Life* (Leicester: IVP, 2009).

Stickleberger, E., *Calvin* (London: James Clarke, 1959).

Thomas, O., tr. J. Aaron, *The Atonement Controversy* (Edinburgh: The Banner of Truth Trust, 2002).

Tuttle, Mark H. (ed.), *Christian History* (issue on Calvin), Vol. V, No. 4 (Worcester, USA: Christian History Institute, 1986).

Wendel, F., *Calvin: The Origins and Development of His Religious Thought* (London: Collins, 1963).

Whelan, R., Baxter C., (eds), *Toleration and Religious Identity: The Edict of Nantes and its implications in France, Britain and Ireland* (Dublin: Four Courts Press, 2003).

2

Moïse Amyraut

With a chapter devoted to Moïse Amyraut, there are many who would dismiss this book as an unwelcome and undesirable contribution to the Calvin Quincentenary. Generally disparaging Amyraldianism as a compromise between Arminianism and Calvinism, they fear a dilution and weakening of what they regard as 'orthodox' Calvinism. However, I believe that sufficient has been written within the last four decades at least to demonstrate that Amyraldian theology is both a reaffirmation of Calvin's original teaching and, more importantly, a confirmation of the true message of the Word of God. Yet, Amyraut continues to have a bad press. In systematic theologies and articles, his distinctive theological stance is usually misrepresented and marginalised. As if the man had openly spurned the Reformation doctrine of Justification by Faith, he is—in some circles at least —having difficulty in shaking off the unflattering epithet of 'the grave digger of the French Reformed Church', a charge repeated as recently as 2003.

Amyraut and Baxter

For the vast majority of students of church history and Christian biography, the Huguenot Amyraut (1596–1664) is an unknown figure compared with someone like his near-contemporary, the Puritan Richard Baxter (1615–91). Yet within a British historical context, Richard Baxter is generally regarded as the chief exponent of Amyraldianism. Even though, at one time, Baxter's doctrinal distinctives were identified as 'Baxterianism', he tends to be styled as an 'Amyraldian'. Who then is the Frenchman whose teaching gave our English Baxter his theological identity? As we all should know, the Puritan is far from being a shadowy figure. His extraordinary ministry in seventeenth-century Kidderminster is celebrated by an appropriate local statue; his nationwide influence was diffused by such still-gripping page turners as *The Saints' Everlasting Rest* and *Call to the Unconverted;* and his lovely hymn 'Ye holy angels bright' is still enjoyed by modern worshippers. Neither must we ignore that his colourful and dramatic life is recorded in his autobiography with its exotic Latin title *Reliquiae Baxterianae.* Lastly, Baxter made a further mark on English church history by his courageous stand before the infamous Judge Jeffreys in 1685.

Turning to Moïse Amyraut, while he had an effective pastoral ministry, he never quite turned Saumur upside down, and this charming town in the Loire Valley exhibits no statue to commemorate him. Although he wrote a series of highly-significant theological works, he wrote no devotional or evangelistic classic, neither is a little-known hymn ever sung. Lastly, no *Reliquiae Amyraldianae* exists to perpetuate his memory. Our ignorance is chiefly due more to prejudice than the language and culture barrier, more formidable perhaps to overcome than the geological problems faced by the builders of the Channel Tunnel. On top of the 'foreign' nature of some features of French culture is French religion in general and that of Huguenot history in particular. This is where an almost unknown Englishman comes to our aid. I refer to a certain John Quick, an author only known to students of the later Puritans.

John Quick and the Huguenots

My known passionate affinities with the Huguenots are due neither to Francophilia as such nor to French Protestant ancestry. For all that my roots are English, my interests are self-consciously spiritual and theological. If any precedents are needed for my enthusiasm, I would cite such English nineteenth-century writers as Samuel Smiles and Richard Heath if not the American historian Henry Baird (probably of Scottish descent). All these authors wrote significant accounts of the Huguenots, especially the latter whose comprehensive six-volume history was published between 1880 and 1895. However,

I feel a close affinity with the aforementioned English Presbyterian minister John Quick (1636–1706), the tercentenary of whose death fell in April 2006. This persecuted puritan was the first writer to chronicle and document the Huguenot epic for English readers in an extensive manner. Being both a personally-acquainted commentator on their affairs and a participant in the struggles of English Nonconformity, Quick is a literary 'link man' and part of the broader story at the same time. So, before we take a look at Quick's look at Amyraut, it is necessary to take a 'quick look at Quick'!

The reason for John Quick's inclusion in our story will be apparent from a sketch of his little-known life. He was born at Plymouth in 1636. After graduating at Oxford in 1657 he was ordained at Ermington in Devon in 1659. Along with his illustrious puritan brethren—a more famous contemporary John Flavel (1628–91) ministered at nearby Dartmouth, Quick exercised a faithful and courageous ministry. He served at Kingsbridge with Churchstow and then at Brixton near Plymouth. Undeterred by the Act of Uniformity (1662), he continued to preach. He was arrested during the Lord's Day morning worship on 13 December 1663 and imprisoned at Exeter. At his trial, Quick was nearly acquitted on a technicality. However, since he refused to give up preaching, he was sent to prison. After suffering for a further eight weeks, he was liberated by Sir Matthew Hale. The Bishop of Exeter, Seth Ward then prosecuted Quick for preaching to the prisoners but the Lord's servant was acquitted, his unashamed 'guilt' notwithstanding!

King Charles II's indulgence of 1672 brought a brief respite for the persecuted puritan brotherhood. Quick was licensed to preach at Plymouth. When restrictions were imposed again the following year, he was imprisoned for three months with other nonconformists at the Marshalsea prison in Plymouth. On his release, Quick left the west of England for London. He then travelled to the Netherlands where he became a minister to the English church at Middleburg in 1679. Returning to London two years later, Quick gathered a Presbyterian congregation in a small meeting house in

Middlesex Court, Bartholomew Close, Smithfield. On the eve of less troubled times, his London ministry—'successful to the conversion of many', said Dr Edmund Calamy—was relatively undisturbed. The 'Glorious Revolution' (1688) and the Toleration Act (1689) eventually brought persecution to an end. Known as a 'serious, good preacher' with a 'great facility and freedom in prayer', John Quick continued to serve his people faithfully until his death on 29 April 1706. He was buried in the Dissenters' burial ground at Bunhill Fields. His wife Elizabeth died in 1708. Their only daughter became the wife of Dr John Evans (1680?–1730) who completed the commentary on the Epistle to the Romans in Matthew Henry's immortal *Exposition*.

Historian of the Huguenots

During his early ministry and subsequently, Quick became acquainted with the Huguenot refugees, some of whom landed at his native Plymouth from La Rochelle in 1681—the year the dreadful 'dragonnades' began. Accordingly, wrote Calamy, Quick 'was very compassionate to those in distress; at a great deal of pains and expense for the relief of the poor French Protestants, and his house and purse were almost ever open to them. He was a perfect master of their language, and had a peculiar respect for their churches, upon the account of their sound doctrine and useful discipline, and the noble testimony which they bore to religion by their sufferings'.

Consistent with his personal courage and pastoral gifts, John Quick combined scholarship with zeal for the truth. The blending of these qualities explains his authorship of a work of major Huguenot interest, the *Synodicon in Gallia Reformata*. This pair of fascinating folios was published in 1692.. The work chiefly consists of the proceedings of all the National synods—twenty-nine in all—of the French Reformed Churches from the first held at Paris in 1559 to the last permitted by Louis XIV at Loudun in 1659. Besides an historical introduction, Quick included the Confession of Faith and Discipline of the Reformed Churches together with the Edict of Nantes (1598) and the Edict of Fontainebleau (1685) commonly known as the 'Revocation of the Edict of Nantes'. Pope Innocent XI's congratulatory letter to the French king is also included along with an account of the dreadful persecution of the immediate post-revocation period. The author's title-page claim—'A work never before extant in any language'—is noteworthy. A French 'edition' was later published at the Hague in 1710 by Jean Aymon. Unlike Aymon, Quick had direct access to original manuscript material borrowed from Huguenot refugees which he then collated and translated. Aymon then re-translated Quick's work back into French—which explains his repetition of some of Quick's inaccuracies! The *Synodicon* remains therefore a primary English source for Huguenot information during the early modern period.

Quick's interest in the Huguenots did not end with the *Synodicon*. Besides a few published sermons of his own, he also prepared for publication a selection of fifty brief—some quite lengthy— biographies of eminent pastors, theologians and martyrs of the French Reformed churches, the *Icones Sacrae Gallicanae*. He also produced a similar selection of twenty Puritans, the *Icones Sacrae Anglicanae*. These ambitious ventures failed with the death in 1700 of William Russell, Duke of Bedford (the dedicatee of the *Synodicon*) who had offered to finance the project. Advancing illness also prevented Quick from collecting subscriptions for the work. Following the author's death, the manuscript volumes were eventually deposited at what is now known as Dr Williams's Library. There they remain in their unpublished state although, since the originals decayed with time, a transcription was made of them in the nineteenth century by the Revd Hugh Hutton, MA, minister of Churchgate Presbyterian Church, Bury St Edmunds. The work took three years (1862–5), for which the then princely sum of £150 was paid!

Quick's life of Amyraut

This brings us to the thirty-fifth of Quick's fifty Huguenot biographies or *Icones*: 'The Life of Mons[r]. Amyraut, Pastor and professor in the Church and University of Saumur'. Interestingly, in the two major studies of Amyraut during the last fifty years by Dr Brian G. Armstrong and Dr Frans Pieter van Stam, this work was neglected. While Quick's *Synodicon* is frequently cited, his *Icones Sacrae Gallicanae* are ignored. However, biographical information is cited from Pierre Bayle's *Dictionnaire historique et critique* (1696), described by Armstrong as 'an under-valued and under-used source containing much that is still important and not readily accessible elsewhere'. For information about Amyraut, Bayle states that his source was 'the memoirs communicated by M. Amyraut the son', a source also used by Quick. However, the latter's biography includes more personal features than Bayle revealed in his *Dictionnaire*. These generally unknown 'personal features' are a vital part of this presentation of Amyraut's life.

His ancestors coming originally from Alsace and later Orleans, Moïse Amyraut was born in September 1596 at Bourgueil in Anjou, a small town in the Loire Valley 40 km west of Tour. Provided an education in the humanities, his father sent him to study law at the university of Poitiers. Proving himself a diligent student working daily for 14 hours, Moïse graduated Licentiate after a year. Travelling home via Saumur, he visited M. Bouchereau, pastor of the Reformed Church, who recognised the young man's extraordinary abilities and piety. Being introduced to the Governor of Saumur, the famous Huguenot soldier-statesman and scholar The Lord Philippe du Plessis-Mornay, young Moïse was encouraged to abandon law and study theology. At first reluctant, his father agreed with the advice given. Studying other works by Tully, Demosthenes and Aristotle, Moïse felt drawn to theology and the Christian ministry through reading John Calvin's *Institutes of the Christian Religion*. He was admitted to the Reformed Academy at Saumur, founded by Lord du Plessis-Mornay in 1599. Moïse thus came under the influence of the Scottish theologian John Cameron (c. 1580–1625) who served as Professor of Theology from 1618–21. Cameron had a profound influence on Moïse who became his most famous pupil. Succeeding the Dutch Francis Gomarus at Saumur, Cameron challenged the ultra-orthodox theology of Calvin's successor Theodore Beza. Restless and outspoken, he became known as 'Bezae mastyx' or 'Beza's scourge'. Effectively signalling a return to the balanced biblicism of Calvin, Amyraut embraced and developed Cameron's 'authentic Calvinism', a *via media* between Arminianism and Bezaism. Such was Amyraut's admiration for Cameron that he imitated his gestures and even spoke French with a Scottish accent!

Pastor & Professor at Saumur

Little information is available about Amyraut for the years 1618–26. However, in 1626, he was called to succeed his life-long friend and former fellow student Jean Daillé as pastor at Saumur. Having commenced his ministry in the town in 1625, Daillé—the future preacher *par excellence*—was called to the great Reformed Temple at Charenton near Paris where he exercised a powerful and influential ministry until his death in 1670. Having authored his first major publication *A Treatise Concerning Religions* (1631), Amyraut was appointed as theology professor in the Academy in 1631. He joined the learned Hebraist Louis Capell and fellow theologian Josué de la Place on the faculty. All three being disciples of Cameron, they exhibited a remarkable harmony 'as is rarely to be met with in academic land' says Bayle. Writing more quaintly, Quick states that 'it was commonly said of them, that their three heads were covered with one bonnet, i. e. with one and the same nightcap'.

Before we proceed, it is important to remember the religious and political context in which the Huguenots lived. While they were a sizeable and significant minority, their liberties within Roman Catholic France were defined by the Edict of Nantes, granted during the reign of Henri IV in 1598. After decades of religious conflict, the Edict guaranteed a degree of religious freedom and other public privileges. However, due to constant intrigue by the Jesuits and other Roman Catholic conservatives, the position of the Huguenots still made them vulnerable. As 'second class citizens', they enjoyed a fragile and frequently-violated peace. To practise the Reformed religion always demanded a combination of courage and wisdom. Throughout their public lives and ministries, the Huguenot pastors generally proved exemplary in this respect. It was during the National Synod of Charenton (1631) that Amyraut made his initial mark. Contrary to earlier custom, the Reformed delegates from the previous National Synod of Castres (1626) presented their complaints and grievances over violations of the Edict of Nantes before King Louis XIII *on their knees*. Determined to honour the King yet maintain their privileges as servants of Christ, Amyraut insisted that he would address His Majesty *standing*. Thus commissioned by the Synod, so he did. In fact, so impressive was Amyraut's demeanour in the whole matter, his courage, manners and integrity won him the esteem of Cardinal Richelieu.

Controversy over predestination

Amyraut is chiefly remembered for setting the cat among the pigeons over the theology of predestination. When a Roman Catholic nobleman—otherwise sympathetic to the Reformed Faith—expressed doubts about what he perceived to be Calvin's teaching, Amyraut responded with his first work on the subject. However, his *Brief Treatise on Predestination* (1634) aroused the wrath of the Reformed world when he expounded a position on election, the extent of the atonement and 'universal grace' at odds with accepted wisdom. Starting what Bayle described as a 'kind of civil war among the Protestant divines of France', it soon became clear that Amyraut—heavily influenced by Calvin—was pursuing a very different theological agenda from 'orthodox' theologians like the 'French John Owen' Pierre du Moulin, but one that was not exposed to many of the *biblical* objections raised by many then and subsequently.

Amyraut and Calvin's Calvinism

Rooted in a dualistic conception of the divine will (see *Deuteronomy 29:29*), Calvin taught that Christ was offered as the Redeemer of the whole world according to God's 'revealed' conditional will albeit only received by elected believers according to God's 'hidden' absolute will. Notwithstanding the rationally-challenging paradox involved, Calvin maintained the doctrines of universal atonement and divine election side by side. Faced by clear biblical evidence for both, he refused to tamper with the scriptural texts.

Logic was not allowed to dictate one emphasis at the expense of the other. Typical of his numerous statements on the extent of the atonement, Calvin commented thus on Romans 5:18: 'Paul makes grace common to all, not because it in fact extends to all, but because it is offered to all. Although Christ suffered for the sins of the world, and is offered by the goodness of God without distinction to all men, yet not all receive him'.

Unhappy with this kind of dualism, Calvin's rationalistic successor Theodore Beza deleted the 'universal' aspect of Calvin's scheme in favour of limited atonement, which in turn provoked the equally-rationalistic Jakob Arminius to delete the 'particular' aspect of Calvin's scheme in favour conditional election. Unimpressed by either of the two deviants, Amyraut was persuaded that Calvin's original position alone possessed biblical integrity. For him, the only option was Calvin's 'authentic Calvinism'. Amyraut also insisted that Calvin's view, with its unique 'mind and heart-set', had enormous pastoral and evangelistic advantages. Roger Nicole admits that Calvin's comment on Romans 5:18 'comes perhaps closest to providing support for Amyraut's thesis'. Even Richard Muller admits that 'Calvin's teaching was ... capable of being cited with significant effect by Moïse Amyraut against his Reformed opponents'. According to Dr Van Stam, at a time when Bezan ultra-orthodoxy had replaced Calvin's balanced biblicism, 'Amyraut...revealed the attraction which the theology of Calvin held for him. He demonstrated this preference in an array of books, in the process proving his familiarity with the writings of this reformer. ... Amyraut rediscovered Calvin, as it were, and was perhaps the Calvin-expert of the day. In any case, Amyraut fell under the spell of Calvin's theology'. Thus historian Philip Benedict—who incorrectly imagines the Canons of the Synod of Dort (1618–19) to represent a *higher* orthodoxy than is the case—recognises Amyraut's position in France accurately when he says that 'the theologians of the Academy of Saumur ... consciously opposed Beza and appealed to Calvin instead. ... In effect they reversed the steps that had been taken in the passage from Calvin to Calvinism'.

Amyraut at Alençon

Amyraut's impeccable *authentic* Calvinist orthodoxy did not shield him from the charge of Arminianising heresy, even though he claimed an orthodoxy consistent with the Canons of Dort. He—with his fellow pastor Paul Testard of Blois who had also published a similarly 'heretical' piece—was tried and acquitted at the National Synod of Alençon (1637). The controversy was to rumble on for decades, not only in France but throughout Europe and beyond. Even today, ultra-orthodox blood pressure is often raised when anyone dares to defend and expound the tenets of Moïse Amyraut. Sadly, for most students of French church history, knowledge of Amyraut is confined to his theological notoriety. Since these theological issues are discussed in depth elsewhere, we will continue to explore the less-familiar features of Amyraut's life.

Returning home from the Synod of Alençon, all Saumur rejoiced at Amyraut's acquittal. The Academy flourished for many years with many students attending from all parts of France and beyond. Indeed, the Saumur Academy became the premier institution of its kind. Amyraut's personal reputation grew with the years, not least among the Roman Catholics. As we have noted, the King's chief minister Cardinal Richelieu greatly admired him.

No compromise

What is striking is the way Amyraut maintained his Reformed convictions without compromise. Surrounded as the Reformed community in France was by a large and not always benign Roman Catholic majority, tensions were not always easy to handle, even during the 'golden years' (1629–61). However, in the true spirit of the Gospel, Amyraut avoided the extremes of social hostility and a servile ecumenism. He demonstrated this when, to ingratiate himself at Rome, the Cardinal advanced a scheme to unite the Roman and Reformed communions in France. He commissioned the Jesuit Father Audebert to sound out the Reformed pastors. Intending to engage in talks with Amyraut, the Jesuit visited Saumur. Brought together by the King's Lieutenant, M. Villeneuve, Father Audebert soon discovered that Amyraut was quite inflexible.

Regarding unity, the latter declared 'That this was a thing more to be wished than hoped for; that the opinions of both were so opposite that there was no probability nor possibility of concerting and adjusting them'. When the Jesuit indicated that the Roman Catholics were ready to abandon the invocation of saints, the merit of good works, purgatory and papal supremacy, Amyraut was not to be taken in. These concessions were too few if they did not include the doctrine of the real presence in the Mass. At this point the Romanist refused to yield. Amyraut concluded the discussion insisting that without this, any unity was 'mere vanity'.

Amyraut's 'authentic Calvinism'

Doctrinal debate over the doctrines of grace involved Amyraut in further controversy in the 1640s. When the English Arminian Samuel Hoard, Rector of Morton in Essex published an attack on predestination, the impact of the work was also felt in France. Just as the English 'proto-Amyraldian' John Davenant replied to Hoard, so did Amyraut. It is fascinating to discover that both authors did not refute Hoard from a *Bezan* perspective. They were conscious of doing so as 'authentic Calvinists'. Amyraut could not have been more explicit in calling his reply *A Defence of the Doctrine of Calvin*. Armstrong states that in this work, 'Amyraut clearly identifies his own teaching with that of Calvin. Of all his writings, this is the most important in demonstrating the distinctives of Amyraldianism as compared to the scholastic orientation of the orthodox'. Persisting in the same stance that produced the heresy trial at Alençon in 1637, it was inevitable that Amyraut's critics would try to make more trouble for him at the next National Synod at Charenton in 1644–5. As before, all attempts to discredit him proved fruitless. Doubtless influenced by Amyraut's criticisms of Islam in his first major work, this synod drew up a liturgy for receiving converted Muslims into membership of the Reformed Churches.

This synod provides us with a glimpse of Amyraut's magnanimous nature when he defended his Saumur colleague Josué de la Place's views over the doctrine of imputed guilt. Properly speaking, Amyraut defended his friend's right to hold such a view (which again can claim some degree of precedent in Calvin!) even though he entertained some reservations about it at the time. He simply did not consider it sufficiently fundamental to dispute about publicly, and his eloquence won the day.

More important to his ongoing ministry among the churches, Amyraut was asked to write a 'paraphrase or commentary' on the Bible. He commenced this in 1644 with his commentary on Romans. Eventually he covered all the epistles, the Acts of the Apostles and the Gospel of John. He died before attempting a harmony of the Gospels. Like Calvin, he declined to do anything on the Book of Revelation.

Compassionate pastor

Personal tragedy hit the Amyrauts in 1645 when their only daughter died at the age of nineteen. To comfort his distressed wife, Amyraut wrote his *Treatise on the State of Believers after Death*. Not initially intended for publication, it was only printed when others, impressed by the therapeutic quality of the work, urged him to do so. Published in 1646, it was translated into English and German. In this work, Amyraut the theologian was also Amyraut the pastor. Combining faithful exegesis with deep sympathy, he was able to minister effectively to the bereaved.

Amyraut was remarkable for the way he combined academic concerns and pastoral compassion. Many besides his students sought his wise solutions to their intellectual and personal perplexities. The Roman Catholics of Saumur knew that when students of their college had disputes with those of the Reformed Academy, they could rely on Amyraut to be a reliable umpire. He was famous for his philanthropy to the poor, irrespective of religious affiliation. When the local monastery was burned down, the friars asked him to approach M. Hervart, the King's Controller of Revenue—who happened to be a Reformed man—to help with rebuilding costs. Quick tells us that 'the begging friars would be sure to knock at his doors, for they never missed of a good alms, their knapsacks being well filled. And he would tell them pleasantly, that he gave them candles that they might read more and study better'.

Quick provides a challenging and beautiful picture of Amyraut the model pastor:

The poor of both religions loved and reverenced him as their common father, for he distributed his charity indifferently among them all. But yet he had a most particular concern for the sick, and how many and urgent so ever his businesses were, they should never dispense with him from visiting them on their beds of languishing, and administering spiritual physic, counsels and comforts suitable to their conditions and inward circumstances. He evaded not this office and service of love, neither for the sultry heats of the day, nor for the storms and bitter colds of the night. He hath quitted his own bed and repose to console dying persons'.

Fidelity to the Reformed Faith

As we discover the gracious character of Moïse Amyraut, it is important to repeat that he always maintained his Reformed convictions without compromise. For him, a compassionate heart and a sound head were not—as is often the case today—mutually exclusive. He proved this in June 1646 when, by order of the Privy Council, during the Roman Catholic Festival of Corpus Christi, the Reformed families of Saumur were ordered to hang tapestries from their balconies as the idolatrous procession passed along the streets of the town. For Amyraut, this situation was a test case for Reformed fidelity. Responding to the instruction of the Seneschal—the chief judge of the city—that Amyraut should direct the Protestant people to obey the order, we see evidence of old-fashioned Calvinist courage. Quick's account reveals something of the drama and tension involved:

[Amyraut] had indeed always preached up subjection unto the higher powers, but then it was in those matters in which conscience was not interested nor concerned, that he was so far from exhorting his flock to yield obedience in this case, that he would go immediately unto every house of the Reformed, and particularly charge them not in the least to obey this wicked order, nor in any wise to yield the least consent unto it, whatever they might suffer for it. And that he would be the first to give them an example and pattern of steadfastness and constancy, and patience in their religion. What he said he did. M. Amyraut was as good as his word. For he was not a reed shaken with the wind; but fixed and immovable in his holy purpose and resolutions as a rock. He therefore quits the High Priest's Hall, the Seneschal's house, and goes from house to house, admonishing and warning all his flock not to have to do in any wise with this idolatry. God's glory and the everlasting salvation of their precious souls were now at stake. They should quit themselves as men, as the ancient saints of God had done before them, rather suffer than sin, burn in the furnace than bow the knee to the King's golden image or impious decree.

Such was the example of one decried as 'the grave digger of the French Reformed Church'!

The Corpus Christi episode illustrates the dilemma constantly facing the Huguenots. In their obedience to the Word of God, they always sought to 'Fear God' and 'Honour the King' (*1 Peter 2:17*). In matters not involving religious conformity they endeavoured to be model subjects. Thus far they were happy to be 'politically correct'. However, should the King command anything contrary to their consciences as Reformed Christians, Peter's bold stand was theirs also: 'We ought to obey God rather than men' (*Acts 5:29*). As Amyraut's behaviour made clear, the Huguenot was guided by 'Christian correctness', a stance which in no way could properly be construed as 'revolutionary'. Such was the influential teaching expounded in the final chapter of John Calvin's *Institutes*. While leaving room for the legitimacy of 'popular magistrates' in their *public capacity* to 'curb the tyranny of kings', the duty of *private* Christians is to 'prove our obedience to them, whether in complying with edicts, or in paying tribute' and cooperating in other civil matters.

Anti-revolutionary Huguenots

Faced by royal tyranny, 'private men' must recognise that while 'the Lord takes vengeance on unbridled domination', our obligation is to 'obey and suffer'. A faithful exegete of the Word of God, Calvin clearly had a high view of kingship. Citing 1 Peter 2:17 and Proverbs 24:21, he states that 'under the term honour, [the Apostle Peter] includes a sincere and candid esteem, and [Solomon], by joining the king with God, shows that he is invested with a kind of sacred veneration and dignity'. Even when rulers are unjust, 'this feeling of reverence, and even of piety, we owe to the utmost of our rulers, be their characters what they may'. This teaching explains why, after the execution of King Charles I in 1649, Huguenots like Amyraut distanced themselves from the English Puritan regicides. Agreeing with Calvin, Amyraut published his treatise *The Sovereignty of Kings* in 1650. At a time when the political heritage of the United Kingdom is fast becoming an 'anything-goes' 'PC' democratic tyranny, no less hostile to Christians than the monarchical tyrannies of old, the teaching of Calvin and Amyraut is worthy of sober reflection today. Surely, the ultimate issue is not 'monarchy *versus* democracy' but the value consensus shared by both the governors and the governed within society, whatever theory of government operates at any one time.

Because of the religious affinities between the Huguenots and the Puritans (especially the Presbyterians), the English civil war created problems in France. Reformed believers were suspected of fomenting revolution against established order. Unlike England, France had already endured the sixteenth-century wars of religion, and, for Amyraut and his generation, the terrible siege of La Rochelle (1627–8) in which Cardinal Richelieu crushed Protestant political power in France forever, was very recent history. In another work, *An Apology for those of the Reformed Religion,* Amyraut took the view that for all that was noble in Huguenot resistance to royal tyranny, just religious grievances were too often mixed up with dubious politics.

Amyraut and monarchy

These issues were brought into sharp focus during the civil disturbances in France known as the War of the Fronde (1648–53). Succeeding Cardinal Richelieu on his death in 1642 (and Louis XIII died the following year), Cardinal Mazarin's unpopular rule was challenged by the Paris Parlement which sought to limit royal power during the minority of Louis XIV. The revolt being suppressed by the Duke of Condé, he himself led a rebellion in 1650 which ended three year later. The entire conflict was civil rather religious, being doubtless influenced by events in England.

So when Condé used his protestant ancestry to gain Huguenot support in 1651, he was disappointed. Amyraut and his brethren preached obedience to the young King. Their allegiance was considered decisive. Count Harcourt summed up the situation when he declared to the deputies of Montauban, "The crown was tottering on the King's head, but you have steadied it."

Returning from banishment, Cardinal Mazarin was no less grateful to the 'little flock'. In 1652, Louis expressed appreciation for Huguenot support: "Our subjects aforesaid of the Pretended Reformed Religion have afforded us sure proofs of their affection and faithfulness, ... wherewith we are much pleased." The King also promised to guarantee the Huguenot privileges provided in the Edict of Nantes. Thus the Huguenots rejoiced. Unlike the English Puritans, they had few misgivings about royalty. At that time, there was no reason to suspect that young Louis would one day become a monster persecutor. However, from 1656 onwards, Louis began to exhibit signs of a change of heart, an intolerant 'absolutist' disposition which eventually led to the terrible Dragonnades of 1681 and Revocation of the Edict of Nantes in 1685.

Amyraut became closely involved with the events of these tumultuous times. In January 1651, the Royal Court came to Saumur. According to custom, there was great pressure on the Reformed community to alter their weekly worship routine during the first three days of the royal visit. Amyraut was prepared to be accommodating on the understanding that their normal Lord's Day services would take place as usual. John Quick provides a fascinating account of what happened next:

> The King came to Saumur the Monday night, and there was no sermon on Wednesday, but on the next Lord's Day the whole service was performed as usual. M. Amyraut preached in the afternoon. The King was just then got into his majority [actually his fourteenth year], and together with several young Lords walked out onto the tennis court, which was near adjoining unto the Temple of the Reformed. The Protestants were then singing the Psalm. The King being a perfect stranger to this action and melody demanded the meaning of it. Somebody answered it was part of the religious worship of the Huguenots. "Let's go in," said the King, "and see what they are

doing." But some great ones then about him obstructed his resolution, and conducted him to his sports and divertisements.

One wonders what might have transpired in the soul of young Louis XIV had he come under the ministry of M. Amyraut. Quick continues:

> Whilst the King was engaged in his play, some of the courtiers had the curiosity to get into the Temple, and the patience to tarry out the whole sermon. M. Amyraut preached upon those words of St Peter, 'Fear God. Honour the King' [*1 Peter 2:17*]. When the action was ended, they declared their great satisfaction one unto the other, and commended the preacher highly, as a man of singular merit and eloquence. They went directly from the Temple to the racket court, and acquainted His Majesty with that excellent discourse of the Huguenot minister; yea and at night when Her Majesty [the Queen Mother] sat at table she was recreated with the punctual relation of it.

Surprise at Amyraut's preaching is not difficult to explain. Roman Catholic propaganda created the impression that the Huguenots were a perpetual threat to church and state. Confronted by the reality of Huguenot piety, those in a position to judge for themselves were able to draw a different conclusion.

Amyraut and Mazarin

Arriving at Saumur the following week, even Cardinal Mazarin heard about the sermon and wanted to meet the preacher. Meeting at the Cardinal's lodgings, the two men sat by the fire and talked. When Amyraut assured Mazarin of Huguenot support for the King, the Cardinal was surprised and charmed at the manners and wisdom of the Reformed Pastor. A day or two later, while the King was on a hunting trip, the Cardinal visited the nearby Abbey of St Bennet. On returning from his walk, which provided a panoramic view of Saumur, he asked his host the Count of Comminges where the Reformed Academy was. The Count pointing it out in the distance, the Cardinal wished to call on Amyraut. Welcomed at the college gate, he was invited to inspect the library. They discussed the Edict of Nantes and the perpetual obligation of the Kings of France to honour it. News of this encounter was the talk of the town. Many were asking what the Cardinal and the Professor discussed. They did not discuss theological differences on this occasion, as Amyraut later made clear. The Count of Guilaut said to the Queen Mother that had they discussed religion, the Cardinal would have more than met his match in M. Amyraut.

Clearly, the Court and the Cardinal were impressed by the piety, learning and integrity of Amyraut. However, while they could not dismiss the Reformed Faith, time was to prove that their hearts remained hostile to the Gospel thus adorned by Amyraut and his brethren.

Amyraut and Jean Daillé

In the meantime, the Reformed Churches continued to flourish and the pastors enriched one another by periodic fellowship. In 1653, Jean Daillé called at Saumur on his way from Paris to La Rochelle to ordain his son Adrien at the Reformed Temple. Quick reminds us that, since their student days, Amyraut and Daillé had remained 'dear friends'. Regarded as the greatest French preacher since Calvin, Daillé had fully supported his friend in his theological conflicts. Both men owed so much to their benefactor, The Lord du Plessis-Mornay. During this meeting, they enjoyed rich fellowship as guests of the godly noble Lord's grandson Lord de Villarnoul at his château at La Forêt-sur-Sèvre in lower Poitou. We may imagine the joys thus shared in the great hall of the château. Quick says that 'their discourses and conversation together did ravish and charm that religious family, and all the guests and strangers that had the happiness to be their auditors'.

Student life at Saumur

Quick also supplies a vivid and charming picture of student life at Saumur. He tells us that 'it was a constant custom with M. Amyraut in the summer evenings to walk in the fields about Saumur, especially after supper. He was always attended with some sixty or fourscore students in divinity, who propounded to him all those difficulties and knotty objections which occurred to them in their private studies'. We can imagine the cut and thrust of provocative yet good-humoured discussion as professor and students fired questions at one another. Quick stresses the importance of these nocturnal excursions:

> These exercises did highly improve those young divines in knowledge, judgement, acumen and ability to defend the truth, and refute errors, and many of them afterwards proved most eminent ministers of the Gospel, and victorious champions of our holy Religion against all the subtle Popish aggressors. And it was these evening walks which occasioned the publication of sundry theological dissertations, which he emitted at diverse times from the press into the open world, and which otherwise might have been buried in the graves of perpetual silence.

Amyaut's accident

In the sharp winter of 1657, Amyraut had a bad fall after leaving the Temple. Carried home in great agony, he was thought to have broken his thigh. All were gravely concerned, including the Roman Catholics, and fear was expressed for his life. As soon as he recovered from shock, 'he began to speak and comfort those that attended him', says Quick, 'telling them that if the Lord should vouchsafe him that favour as to enjoy the benefit of his tongue and understanding to edify his brethren to the last of his life, he should account this the happiest providence which ever had befallen him'.

Amyraut had actually suffered a hip dislocation and torn ligaments. He was out of action for six months, during which time he attended to his voluminous correspondence, continuing also with his paraphrase on the Acts of the Apostles. Becoming more mobile with the aid of crutches, he was carried from place to place in a Sedan chair. At the end of August, accompanied by his daughter-in-law, he visited the small spa town of Bourbon in Burgundy, famous for its attractive vista of the Loire Valley. During his stay, many Reformed believers gathered in his apartment on the Lord's Day for worship, ministry and fellowship. They were 'edified', says Quick, 'by his excellent and fruitful sermons'. One sermon in particular was highly valued. Finding relief from the *eaux de Bourbon*, he drew parallels between the healing effect of the waters and the grace of God in the Gospel.

Amyraut in Paris

Making their way to Paris, Amyraut and his daughter-in-law were welcomed by M. Hervart (the King's Controller of Revenue and a Reformed man) at whose residence they stayed for three months. The Princess of Tarente, the godly daughter of the Huguenot Duke de la Force enjoyed their company and especially Amyraut's discussions on theological and devotional matters. Appearing frequently at the great Temple at Charenton, he preached sermons on the glory of Christ and the work of the Holy Spirit, which were published.

Learning from M. Hervart that Amyraut was in town, Cardinal Mazarin welcomed a further opportunity to speak with the Reformed professor. When they first met, the Cardinal's position during the Fronde had been much less secure. Always impressed by Amyraut's personal integrity and learning, and recalling with pleasure his visit to the Saumur Academy and its library, the Cardinal now invited the Huguenot to see his house and library. While relations were respectful and even cordial, it should be remembered that synodical assemblies of the Reformed Churches could only be approved by the Government. During another visit, having been asked by the Reformed consistory of Paris to petition the Cardinal to authorise a new National Synod, Amyraut duly approached him on the subject. Suspicions about Reformed influence always lurking in the background, matters were never plain sailing. However, the Cardinal, urging Amyraut to be patient, invited him to put the request in writing, which he did.

The last synod

Permission for the National Synod of Loudun was eventually granted. It was to prove the final synod ever allowed by Louis XIV as he increasingly pursued a Jesuit-inspired policy to exterminate the Reformed churches of France. Indeed, the King and his advisers had good reason to respect Huguenot resolve. When the Synod commenced 'by His Majesty's Permission' on 10 November 1659, the King's Commissioner demanded that the Huguenots should be more submissive to His Majesty and less antagonistic to the Church of Rome. The Synod Moderator, the illustrious M. Jean Daillé rose to the occasion. While he affirmed the loyalty and submission of the Reformed churches to the King 'as next under God' in all things lawful, he refused to dilute their theological stance. He bravely affirmed that, 'As to those words *Antichrist*, found in our Liturgy, and *idolatry* and *deceit of Satan*, found in our Confession [of Faith], they be words declaring the grounds and reasons of our separation from the Romish Church, and doctrines which our fathers maintained in the worst of times, and which we are fully resolved as they, through the aids of Divine grace, never to abandon, but to keep faithfully and inviolably to the last gasp'.

It is interesting to note that John Quick was writing his biography of Amyraut in 1696, eleven years after the Revocation of the Edict of Nantes (1685). Looking back wistfully, he wrote of the Synod of Loudun: 'I pray God, it may not be their last. It being six and thirty years since it was broken up [10 January 1660], and the churches in that kingdom are all ruined and desolate'. The next synod was planned (DV) for Nîmes in 1662/3, but it was never to be. However, according to the amazing providence of 'the wonderful Numberer', and nine years after Quick's death, the next took place in the Cévennes in 1715, the very year Louis XIV died. But that is another and happier story!

Reformed Faith and Order

It is appropriate here to mention that synods had a vital place in the life of the Reformed churches of France. Respectful and courteous to both Anglican and Roman Catholic churchmen, they remained committed to Reformed Faith *and* Order. Indeed, the Huguenots were as tenacious over their 'Order' as they were over their 'Faith'. Amyraut believed with Calvin and Beza that, according to clear New Testament teaching, 'elder' and 'bishop' were terms relating to one and the same individual, as surely as 'elder' and 'deacon' denoted quite different roles (see *1 Tim. 3; Tit.*

1). He also taught that each church should be governed by a plural body or council of elders, that such a 'consistory' was made up of 'Ministers of the Word' and 'ruling elders' (*Acts 20:17, 28; 1 Tim. 5:17*). Showing little sympathy for congregational independency, he also believed that synods had divine warrant (*Acts 15*). They enabled churches to express connexional fellowship and solidarity. However, while French Reformed Church Order stated that provincial synods were to be 'subordinate' to national synods, it was only a 'self-subordination'. By referring to their 'churches' in plural terms, their approach was 'bottom-up' rather than 'top-down' as in the Presbyterian Church [singular] hierarchical system. Amyraut had already published a work on church order before the National Synod of Loudun. At the Synod, he was commissioned to prepare a treatise showing the 'Conformity' of the discipline of the Reformed Churches of France with the 'ancient primitive Church'. Dying before this work was finished, it was completed by his pupil Matthieu Larroque, Pastor of Quevilly near Rouen, whose treatise was later translated into English.

A faithful friend

As in England, where Anglicans regarded non-episcopally-ordained Puritans as not true ministers, so the French Roman Catholic clergy dismissed the orders of the Huguenot ministers. Ever concerned to combine courtesy with tenacity, Amyraut put his theory of church order to good use. When M. Perrefix, Archbishop of Paris visited Saumur, he requested a meeting with Amyraut. Knowing the scriptural prohibition against bishops (= elders!) being 'lords' (*1 Peter 5:3*), Amyraut refused to address Roman Catholic bishops as 'My Lord' unless they were peers of the realm (itself an arrangement the Huguenots were hardly in a position to correct). Once the Archbishop—not being a peer—realised he would only be addressed as 'Mr', he agreed to an unofficial private meeting with Amyraut. While he was quite a civil man, he was possibly tinged with jealousy where the Parisian preacher Jean Daillé was concerned. Quick's revealing report is not without a touch of humour:

They spent together in that conversation about three hours,

discoursing of the affairs of the great world, and the most eminent persons for learning and religion in the communion of both churches. This led them into a discourse of M. Daillé, a person of extraordinary parts and famous for his profound knowledge in the learned world. M. Amyraut observed that the Archbishop always spoke of him slightingly, and by the single name of Daillé; which made M. Amyraut never to mention him without a preface and title of honour.

Faith and good works

We have thus noticed that in those tense and potentially-explosive times, Amyraut was concerned to combine tenacity of conviction with courtesy and compassion. A beautiful example of the latter occurred in 1662, two years before he died. Following a bad harvest that year, there was a great shortage of corn in France. Due to her wise management, Mme Amyraut had—Joseph-like—stocked up large reserves of corn at their country house in the Vale of Anjou. Says Quick, 'She had stacked it up in the barns and fields for sundry years of plenty together most abundantly'. Urged to take financial advantage of the situation by selling the corn, the Amyrauts refused to follow what they construed as selfish and ungodly advice. Instead, while taking prudent care of his family and servants should bad harvests continue, they drew up a plan to distribute the corn freely to the poor, irrespective of religious persuasion. Observing Paul's directive to 'do good to all, especially to those who are of the household of faith' (*Galatians 6:10*), first the Reformed poor, then the Roman Catholic poor benefited from their gracious generosity. Quick writes that 'the Roman Catholics whose hungry bellies and empty bowels were refreshed by him, loved and honoured him, calling him the common father of the poor, declaring that in his charities he made no distinction between them and those of his own religion'.

Amyraut's final illness

At the commencement of the September vacation in 1663, the Amyrauts retired to their country house as usual. Within days Moïse became unwell, developing a high but intermittent fever. Instead of returning to Saumur for medical help, he stayed to enjoy a well-deserved rest. After several weeks, his condition deteriorating, Amyraut bowed to the inevitable and returned to Saumur. Concern for his health grew and the sad news spread rapidly. Many anxious visitors called to see him, Roman Catholics as well as Reformed people. As his end drew near, he testified of his faith to a captive audience crowded around his bed. So moving were his last hours that Quick referred to Amyraut's death-bed utterances in a later funeral sermon. He did so to prove the dying man's fidelity to the Reformed Faith to the last:

> [He proved] the truth of the Christian religion, and of our Holy Reformed religion, by many unanswerable arguments. "This I have professed," said he; "I have preached this Holy Reformed religion well nigh forty years." And turning himself unto the Papists (for there were many then present in his chamber, spectators and witnesses of his last end) "Gentlemen," said he, "This is the only true religion, and out of it there is no salvation. That God to whom I am going knows that I do speak the very truth." This, and much more he uttered with a clear and audible voice; yea, and those very Papists heard him with much reverence and attention.

He lingered several days, during which time many of his flock received their beloved pastor's final exhortations. Quick adds this further moving information:

> He had advised them to stand steadfast in the faith, and to hold fast to their profession without wavering, and to prepare against the evil times of sore trials which were approaching, for the God of judgement was at the door, and heavy judgements would begin at the house of God, and therefore how painful soever their cross and sufferings might be, they should not faint, nor prevaricate in, nor apostatise from their holy religion. For he protested to them in the presence of God to whose tribunal he was now a going, that it was the only true one in the whole world, and that out of it there was no salvation to be obtained. I say, after he had given them these and a great many other divine counsels, he blessed them in the name of the Lord'.

Faithful to the end

The dying servant of God clearly foresaw the coming persecutions which afflicted the Reformed churches of France two decades later. He had sufficient strength to repeat some of these exhortations to another pastor from Poitou who, passing through Saumur and hearing that Amyraut was dying, called to see him. Encouraging his rather diffident brother, Amyraut said: 'The doctrine I have taught my scholars in the university and my church in the city is the very truth of God, by which we must all be saved'.

After giving his son directions about his will, Amyraut said farewell to his wife and family. Quick describes his last moments thus:

> In the fifteen last moments of his life, he joined his hands together, and lifted them up with his eyes unto heaven, waiting as dying Jacob did for God's salvation. And in that posture breathed out his blessed soul into the arms of his Redeemer'.

And so this honoured servant of Christ died on the 18 January 1664, aged sixty-eight years. His dearly beloved wife, who also became ill during her husband's sickness, survived him by only a few months. Their son—whose own son Moses eventually settled here—met John Quick in London after escaping to England at the time of the Revocation of the Edict of Nantes. Quick describes him as a man 'of serious piety, being an illustrious confessor of our Lord Jesus in these woeful times of tribulation'. He later served as an Advocate in the High Court of Justice in the Hague. After presenting an engraving of his father to one of the greatest of Amyraut's pupils, Pierre du Bosc—Minister of the Reformed Church at Caen in Normandy and described by Louis XIV as the greatest orator in France—the eminent pastor added to the portrait a personal Latin tribute to his professor. Thus translated, this worthy epitaph reads:

> From Moses down to Moses, none,
> Among the sons of men,
> With equal lustre ever shone,
> In manners, tongue and pen.

Is it any wonder that Richard Baxter should be impressed by this man whose books he so much admired? Indeed, is it so dubious a privilege after all to be dubbed an Amyraldian?

Postscript

AMYRAUT, APOSTASY AND THE REVOCATION (1685)

As I argue in my *Calvinus* (see below), recent research confirms the absurdity of linking the supposed debilitation of French Calvinism to Amyraldianism. Abjuration statistics give an entirely contrary picture, especially where the pastors were concerned. Since Amyraut's influence was greatest north of the Loire, it is a striking fact that pastors were generally more faithful in the northern provinces where 8 per cent abjured compared with 18 per cent in the 'high orthodox' southern provinces. In particular, the province of the Ile-de-France lost 4 per cent compared with 27 per cent in the Cévennes and 41 per cent in Béarn. It is significant that in the north, unlike the south, the smaller protestant population owed its strength more to personal conviction than to nominal adherance. Contrary to the fears of their high orthodox critics, the Amyraldian pastors still combined an eirenic spirit with a decided aversion to Roman Catholic dogma. If their Calvinism was kinder and less socially aggressive, their theological commitment was unquestioned, even if, for various 'worldly-wise' reasons, apostasies were not uncommon among their adherents. To blame Amyraut for facilitating easy defections to Rome among the Reformed is a travesty of truth.

Further reading:

Armstrong, B. G., *Calvinism and the Amyraut Heresy: Protestant Scholasticism and Humanism in Seventeenth-Century France* (Madison: University of Wisconsin Press, 1969)

Amyraut, M., *Traitté des religions contre ceux qui les estiment toutes indifferentes* (Saumur, 1631); English translation full title: *A Treatise Concerning Religions, in Refutation of the Opinion which accounts all indifferent, wherein is also evinced the necessity of a Particular Revelation, And the Verity and preeminence of the Christian Religion above the Pagan, Mahometan, and Jewish rationally Demonstrated* (London, 1660).

——*Brief Traitté de la predestination et de ses principales dependences* (Saumur: Isaac Desbordes, 1634).

——*Defensio doctrinae J. Calvini de absoluto reprobationis decreto* (Saumur: I. Desbordes, 1641).

————*Defense de la doctrine de Calvin* (Saumur: I Desbordes, 1644).

————*Discours de l'estat des fideles apres la mort* (Saumur: J. Lesnier, 1646); tr: *The Evidence of things not seen, or Diverse … Discourses Concerning the State of Good and Holy Men after Death* (London: n.d.).

————*Apologie pour ceux de la Religion Reformeé* (Saumur: I. Desbordes, 1647).

————*Discours sur la souveraineté des rois* (Charenton: L. Vendosme, 1650).

————*Du gouvernement de l'eglise contre ceux qui veulent abolir l'usage & l'autorité des synodes, Avec un appendice au livre du gouvernement de l'eglise où il est traité de la puissance des consistoires* (Saumur: I. Desbordes, 1653; 2nd. ed. 1658).

————*Discours chrestien sur les eaux de Bourbon* (Charenton: A. Cellier, 1658).

————*Cinq sermons prononcez a Charenton* (Charenton: A. Cellier,1658).

————*Deux sermons sur la matiere de la justification et de la sanctification* (Saumur: I. Desbordes, 1658).

————*Theses Salmurienses* (abbr. title, see Armstrong), 4 vols. (Saumur, 1665, Geneva, 1665).

Baird, H. M. *The Huguenots and the Revocation of the Edict of Nantes,* 2 vols. (London: Hodder & Stoughton,1895).

Bayle, P., *The Dictionary Historical and Critical of Mr Peter Bayle, Vol. 1* (London: 1734).

Benedict, P., *The Faith and Fortunes of France's Huguenots, 1600–85* (Aldershot: Ashgate, 2001).

Clifford, A. C., *Atonement and Justification: English Evangelical Theology 1640–1790—An Evaluation* (Oxford: OUP, 1990, 2002).

————*Calvinus: Authentic Calvinism, A Clarification* (Norwich: Charenton Reformed Publishing, 1996; 2nd ed. 2007).

————*Amyraut Affirmed* (Norwich: Charenton Reformed Publishing, 2004).

————Introduction to John Davenant, *A Dissertation on the Death of Christ* (Weston Rhyn: Quinta Press, 2006).

————(ed.), *Christ for the World: Affirming Amyraldianism* (Norwich: Charenton Reformed Publishing, 2007).

Grant, A. J., *The Huguenots* (London: Thornton Butterworth, 1934).

Heath, R., *The Reformation in France* , 2 vols (London: The Religious Tract Society, 1886).

Holt, M. P., (ed.), *Renaissance and Reformation in France* (Oxford: OUP, 2002).

Jenkins, D. L., *Saumur Redux: Josué de la Place & the Question of Adam's Sin* (Harleston, Norfolk: LC Christian Monographs, 2008).

Larroque, M., *The Conformity of the Ecclesiastical Discipline of the Reformed Churches of France with that of the Primitive Christians* (London: 1691).

Muller, R., *The Unaccommodated Calvin* (Oxford: OUP, 2000).

Nicole, R. *Moyse Amyraut (1596–1664) and the Controversy on Universal Grace* (Harvard University thesis, 1966).

Nuttall, G. F., *Richard Baxter and Philip Doddridge: a Study in a Tradition* (London, Dr Williams's Library, 1954).

Pittion, J.-P., 'Intellectual life in the Académie of Saumur, 1633–1685 (Unpublished PhD thesis, Trinity College, Dublin, 1970). This work is currently being prepared for publication.

Prestwich, M., 'The Huguenots under Richelieu and Mazarin, 1629–61: A Golden Age?' in Irene Scouloudi (ed.), *Huguenots in Britain and their French Background, 1550–1800* (London: Macmillan Press, 1987).

Quick, J., article on, see *Dictionary of National Biography* (Oxford: OUP, 1885–)

——*Synodicon in Gallia Reformata* (London: 1692).

——*The Triumph of Faith* (London: 1698).

——*Icones Sacrae Gallicanae:* 'The Life of Mons[r]. Amyraut, Pastor and Professor in the Church and University of Saumur' (1700), MS on deposit at Dr Williams's Library, London, DWL 6, 38–39 (35).

Smiles, S., *The Huguenots—their settlements, churches, and industries in England and Ireland* (London: John Murray, 1880 ed).

——*The Huguenots in France after the Revocation of the Edict of Nantes* (London: Daldy, Isbister & Co, 1875).

Van Stam, F. P., *The Controversy over the Theology of Saumur, 1635–1650: Disrupting Debates among the Huguenots in Complicated Circumstances* (Amsterdam & Maarsen: APA-Holland University Press, 1988).

Wakeman, H. O., *The Ascendancy of France, 1598–1715* (London: Rivingtons, 1959).

Updates 2022

Amyraut, M., tr. Matthew Harding, *Amyraut on Predestination* (Norwich: Charenton Reformed Publishing, 2017).

Baxter, Richard, *Reliquiae Baxterianae or, Mr Richard Baxter's Narrative of the Most Memorable Passages of his Life and Times*, ed. N. H. Keeble, John Coffey. Tim Cooper, and Tom Charlton, 5 vols (Oxford: Oxford University Press, 2020).

——*To Live is CHRIST*, ed. Alan C. Clifford (Norwich: Charenton Reformed Publishing, 2022).

Clifford, A. C., 'Puritans Vindicated' (2012); https://english-reformed-church.co.uk/articles/ (accessed 2022-07-25).

——'The Bartholomew Legacy—remembering the martyrs' (2022): english-reformed-church.co.uk/articles/ (accessed 2022-07-25).

——*John Jones Talsarn: Pregethwr Y Bobl/The People's Preacher* (Norwich: Charenton Reformed Publishing, 2013).

——*Richard Baxter: The Gospel Truth* (Norwich: Charenton Reformed Publishing, 2016).

——'Amyraldian Soteriology and Reformed-Lutheran *rapprochement*' in Balserak, J., West J., (eds.), *From Zwingli to Amyraut: Exploring the Growth of European Reformed Traditions* (Göttingen: Vandenhoek & Ruprecht, 2017).

——*Calamy Celebrated: The 350th Anniversary of the Birth of Dr Edmund Calamy* (H&E Publishing/Andrew Fuller Center for Baptist Studies (Peterborough, Ontario, 2021).

Daniel, Curt, *The History and Theology of Calvinism* (Darlington: EP Books, 2019).

Hartog, Paul A., *Calvin on the Death of Christ: A Word for the World* (Eugene, Oregon: Cascade Books, 2021).

Martin I. Klauber (ed.), *The Theology of the French Reformed Churches: From Henry IV to the Revocation of the Edict of Nantes* (Grand Rapids, Michigan: Reformation Heritage Books, 2014).

Roberts, Llanbrynmair, J., *For Whom did Christ Die? The Designs of the Death of Christ*, ed. Alan C. Clifford (Norwich: Charenton Reformed Publishing, 2014).

Further writings of Richard Baxter, Edmund Calamy, and other nonconformists can be found at quintapress.com/PDF_Books.html

3
Jean Daillé

Regarded by some as France's second Calvin, Jean Daillé, the famous Protestant preacher was born at Chatellerault (25 km north-east of Poitiers) on 6 January 1594. Growing up in a land ravaged by thirty years of religious wars, he was only four years old when the 'Calvinist-turned-Catholic' King Henri IV granted extensive liberties to his former Huguenot friends in the Edict of Nantes (1598). Dying in Paris in 1670, Jean Daillé thus lived and ministered during that period of fragile peace between the granting of the Edict and its revocation by King Louis XIV in 1685.

Observing Jean's great love for books, his father waived the idea of a business career for his son. At eleven years of age, he was sent to St Maixent in Poitou for his primary education. Bereaved early of parents who had suffered much for their Protestantism, an uncle became a diligent and devoted guardian, encouraging his nephew's spiritual stirrings.

Godly scholar

Later Jean studied philosophy and theology at the Reformed academy at Saumur, founded in 1599 by the town's governor, the eminent Huguenot soldier-statesman, Philippe Duplessis-Mornay (1549–1623). In recognition of his remarkable abilities, Daillé was appointed tutor to the governor's two grandsons in 1612. The governor—himself an accomplished scholar—was greatly attached to the future preacher on account of his youthful godliness. Spending many hours together, this protestant Gamaliel completed Daillé's education by imparting his solid biblical wisdom. In 1623 Daillé entered the ministry at M. Duplessis-Mornay's château of

La Forêt-sur-Sèvre in lower Poitou. Shortly after, the Huguenot nobleman died in the arms of the new pastor who then assumed responsibility for the publication of his patron's memoirs.

Powerful preacher

John Quick introduces Jean Daillé as 'the Chrysostom of France', a high commendation indeed. Not surprisingly, Daillé's preaching and pastoral gifts were soon in great demand. In 1625 he was elected pastor of the Reformed church at Saumur. In the following year he was called by the Paris consistory to preach at the large temple at Charenton, where a congregation of several thousands was served by four or five pastors. From this influential centre of French Protestantism, Daillé ministered until his death in 1670. John Quick relates the impact Daillé made in Paris:

> In this most famous church (and in those days one of the chiefest in Reformed Christendom) did the good providence of God grant him a fixed and secure station for the remainder of his life, and here he enjoyed a long continued health, and served the Lord in the ministry no less than four & forty years. The city of Paris was the glorious theatre of the most refined wits of Europe. And upon it, and in their sight and audience did M. Daillé display those rich talents of his polite and recondite learning. None that ever heard or knew him could justly tax him for wrapping them up in a napkin, or hiding his candle under a bushell. For besides that great number of books which he made, and are ample testimony of his laborious diligence in his study, and so received by the whole world, his consistory also will honour him with their most laudable attestations, and epistles of commendation that he performed the ordinary duties of his ministerial function with unwearied pains and constancy, not allowing himself any spare hours to unbend his bow, or divert himself with any innocent recreation. Nor was he interrupted in the course and exercise of his holy calling by reason of his domestical affairs. Yea, he was never absent from his church those four and fourty years in which he was their pastor, but only twice. The first time was in the year 1639, when he went into Poitou, to see his own and his wife's relations. The other journey which he took was fourteen years after, viz. in the year 1653, when he rode unto [La] Rochelle, to ordain his son minister in that [then] flourishing ... Church of Christ.

Published far and wide, his Christ-exalting sermons were appreciated for their clear exegesis, fervent delivery and warm application. Compared with his pastoral colleagues, it was said that Daillé was the only preacher whose voice could be clearly heard anywhere in the great temple. As Quick has made clear, he was a model of ministerial diligence. Daillé was thus regarded by many as the greatest French Reformed preacher and author since John Calvin.

Living in troubled times, Daillé's earthly joys were tempered by national and personal tragedy. His only son Adrien was born on 31 October 1628. On that very day, after three unsuccessful relief attempts by the English navy, the besieged Protestant city of La Rochelle fell to Louis XIII's minister Cardinal Richelieu. That eventful day marked the end of political Protestantism in France. Inviting another comparison with Calvin, Daillé was bereaved of his devoted wife on 31 May 1631 after six years of marriage. He never remarried. Finding solace in the comforts of the Gospel and in greater literary activity, the Lord thus sanctified his servant's sorrows to the greater edification of the Reformed churches.

Daillé was further comforted by a unique bond which developed between father and son. Trained by his father, Adrien (as Quick has related) was called to the pastorate of the Reformed church at La Rochelle in 1653. During this journey (as we noted in the previous chapter), Daillé spent time at Saumur with his friend Amyraut. Following the death of his father's eminent colleague at Charenton, Jean Mestrezat (1592–1657), Adrien was called to serve alongside his father in 1658.

Contender for the Faith

Besides his ever popular sermons, Daillé's books were in great demand. He brilliantly refuted Roman Catholic claims in *A Treatise Concerning the Right use of the Fathers* (1631) and *An Apology for the Reformed Churches* (1633). These works were deeply resented by the Roman clergy in France. Indeed, in the former work, the author makes nonsense of Rome's reliance on early patristic authority. Since disputes between Rome and the Reformed churches involved theological developments of a much later date, e.g. transubstantiation became official only in 1215, the writings of the early fathers provided little help in resolving them. Besides, while dealing with other issues, many of their writings are forged, corrupted, obscure, mistaken, incompetent, self-contradictory and very far from being unanimous! In short, the writings of the Fathers have no place beside inspired and authoritative Scripture.

In the *Apology*, Daillé refutes the Roman charge that Protestants are schismatics, arguing that separation from her errors is an absolute necessity. While stating that differences between Reformed believers do not touch the foundation of faith, differences between Rome and the Reformed do. Drawing attention to the Roman doctrines of image worship, papal supremacy, tradition and the sacrifice of the mass, Daillé concludes: 'It is easy to see that these articles and many others…overthrow the foundations of faith and piety: so that it is not lawful for us to comply with those which hold them.'

When English translations of these works appeared, the Puritans rejoiced in the labours of their Huguenot brother. However, while Daillé's views on authority and churchmanship were welcomed by Presbyterians, many English Episcopalians were no less irritated than their French Roman Catholic counterparts.

While none could doubt Daillé's strong Protestant convictions, moderate French Catholics held him in high esteem for his scholarship, abilities, integrity and wisdom. The Catholic *littérateur* J—L Guez de Balzac (1597–1654) once exclaimed to him, "Oh that such a man as you are were on our side!"

Authentic Calvinist

Daillé was also involved in internal debates among the Reformed churches. He agreed with his friend and former fellow-student, the Saumur academy Professor Moïse Amyraut (1596–1664) that the scholastic high Calvinism then in vogue was a distortion of John Calvin's more biblical teaching. Maliciously misrepresented ever since, the Amyraldians rejected a simplistic doctrine of limited atonement by appealing to the Bible, Calvin and the Canons of Dordt! Despite vindication at the three national Synods of Alençon (1637), Charenton (1644–5) and Loudun (1659–60), Amyraut was attacked by his high orthodox brethren in France and Holland.

Attempting to pacify their anger, Daillé wrote in defense of the synods, continually warning that divisions among the Reformed could be exploited by Rome. He pleaded, "Do not set the house on fire to get rid of a spider!"

Halcyon days

Replete with vivid biblical allusions, John Quick provides a mid-century picture of the character and influence of the Reformed church at Charenton:

> The church of Paris had never been better provided than at that time, for they were the days of grace indeed unto her, when she enjoyed the labours of those five illustrious ministers Daillé, Drelincourt, Le Faucheur, Mestrezat and Aubertin. And the godly judicious Christians were wont to style those days their halcyon days, the sunshine of their prosperity, the years of divine benedictions. For that church did then flourish in her greatest lustre. She looked forth as the morning, fair as the moon, clear as the sun, beautiful as Tirzah, comely as Jerusalem, and terrible as an army with banners. She abounded in the choicest spices, in the richest graces of God's Holy Spirit, and in all the fruits of righteousness unto the praise of His glorious name. She was then a most excellent pattern and example unto all the Reformed churches in Christ in the kingdom, and was renowned throughout the whole world for the sparkling brightness of her faith, and the comforting flames of her charity.

Brave and loyal moderator

During this critical mid-century period, Daillé's edifying ministry and wise counsel helped prepare the Reformed churches of France for the coming persecutions which, fifteen years after his death, culminated in the Revocation of the Edict of Nantes (1685). Always prominent in the national synods of the Reformed churches, he presided at the last synod prior to the revocation which assembled at Loudun in 1659.

In his speech at the synod, the King's Commissioner demanded as usual that the Huguenots should be submissive to His Majesty and less antagonistic to the Church of Rome. While Daillé affirmed the loyalty and submission of the Reformed churches in all things lawful, he refused to dilute their theological stance. He bravely affirmed that, "As to those words *Antichrist*, found in our Liturgy, and *idolatry* and *deceit of Satan,* found in our Confession of Faith, they are the expressions that declare the reasons and the foundation of our separation from the Church of Rome, and the doctrine which our fathers maintained in the most cruel times, and which we are resolved, following their example, by God's grace, never to forsake, but to preserve faithfully and inviolably to the last moment of our lives."

Courageous pastor

Ever ready to contend for the faith, Daillé's personal courage was not confined to the study, the printed page or the pulpit. In 1669, the last year of his life, he was asked to attend the execution of a lapsed Protestant found guilty of murder. Refusing the services of a priest, the man's request for a Protestant pastor was granted by the judge. Sentenced to a barbaric death, his punishment was to be the procedure known as 'breaking on the wheel'. Quick reminds us of the terrible nature of this form of execution:

> [this] miserable fellow lay bound and stretched out upon the wheel, expecting every moment those terrible blows of the iron bar, which would break the bones of his legs, thighs and arms to pieces.

Thousands of noisy Roman Catholics were present to witness the awful spectacle.Seizing the opportunity to preach the Gospel, Daillé courageously made his way to the scaffold. His compassionate ministrations before the now silent Parisian mob happily brought the poor wretch to repentance and faith in Christ. Then, lifting up his powerful voice in prayer, Daillé commended the saved sinner to God before the dreadful sentence was carried out. Quick relates the extraordinary situation:

> All this long discourse was held by him in a public place, in the audience of many thousands of Papists, who most certainly neither loved this Protestant minister nor his religion. Besides, it was a rare sight, and such an one as had never been known nor seen before in that place, a Protestant minister preaching and praying before a world of people. Yet did they all hear him patiently the whole time with a most profound silence.

Undisturbed by the subdued and thoughtful crowd, Jean Daillé then descended the scaffold and returned safely to his house.

Shortly after this incident, the eldest of Daillé's four colleagues, Charles Drelincourt (1595–1669) died. In the following spring, he prepared and preached his Easter sermons. Quick says that

> The subject matter of these two last sermons has something in them worthy of consideration, for it agreed so well with the sad circumstance of the time in which they were preached, that many conceived [that] the minister, having a prophetical foresight of what after did befall him, had chosen those texts of Scripture expressly for the purpose. For can a dying man have any better or more suitable thoughts and meditation than those of the Resurrection of our Lord Jesus, which he handled in the first sermon, and which is the model and pattern of ours? … And the second sermon led him as it were by the hand unto this doctrine and duty, of making a most faithful acknowledgement, and general confession by word of mouth unto God of all His divine favours and mercies, with which He had loaded him continually…

Eternity beckons

A few days later, Daillé seemingly suffered a stroke. He lingered for several days, during which he frequently uttered the words, "For me to live is Christ and to die is gain." Fearing the worst, many of the faithful visited the dying pastor, who was amazingly lucid until just before the end. Besides his son Adrien, his colleague Jean Claude ministered with comforting counsel and prayer. Pierre du Bosc, another Saumur alumni, was also present. Enjoying a prolonged spell of lucidity, the dying preacher ministered to his symathising visitors, as Quick relates:

> And we must not forget in one of his greatest reveries how excellently he did expound and apply those words of Job, "I know that my Redeemer liveth" [*Job 19:25*], from whence he drew an invincible argument to prove the resurrection of this very individual body, which should be eaten by worms, for 'tis certainly true, that he set forth that argument in its fullest colours, and the clearest evidence, and urged it to the utmost.

After commending his family and friends to God, he died on 15 April 1670, aged 76 years. Truly, the end of this eminent preacher and faithful servant of Christ was glorious. His legacy remains to be explored with immense profit. His godly character has much that is worthy of emulation. Like Calvin, Jean Daillé had a penchant for direct speaking, which didn't always go down well. As a man for whom God's truth was everything, he was no 'man pleaser'. Yet, again like Calvin, Daillé also had a 'human' side, as Quick is anxious to remind us:

> His person and conversation were most acceptable, and that silver crown, which God was pleased to put upon his hoary head somewhat early did render him the more venerable. He was easy of access, sweet and familiar in discouse, for he accomodated himself to everyone's capacity and understanding, insomuch that the common people accounted him their preacher, as the most learned and advanced in knowledge accepted him for their doctor.

Humorous Huguenot

Contrary to the bad press some Protestants sadly earn, Daillé was a Calvinist who could smile! Quick reveals more of the humanity of Jean Daillé, on which note we conclude our sketch of his character:

> His piety was neither morose nor sour. For he never believed that mirth and laughter were forbidden by God. He was no enemy to innocent raillery, and those who understood it would say that he had no unbecoming faculty that way, but would be ingenious and tart in his repartee. He was not as many learned men, who when they come out of their libraries and studies are austere and unsociable: no, the very contrary was to be found in him; for when he had been most studious, and spent most hours in reading and meditation, you saw no more of his reservedness. He unbent the bow as he came out of his study, and left behind him all his austerity and melancholy. And yet his books and study were his principal recreation and his chiefest delights.

Before we sample some Daillé sermons, a few comments about two of the ministers who comforted him at the end are in order. Jean Claude (1619–87) became the leading pastor at Charenton after Daillé's death. Three years later, he published his magnificent apologia for the Reformed churches, *La Defense de la Reformation* (*1673*). At the Revocation of the Edict of Nantes twelve years later, Claude courageously stood his ground. Banished from France by Louis XIV, he died in the Netherlands as a refugee pastor at the

Hague in 1687. Pierre du Bosc (1623–92), pastor of the Reformed Church at Caen in Normandy, bravely pleaded with the King not to revoke the Edict. His efforts made a deep but sadly short-lived impression, so much so that Louis XIV described him as the greatest orator in France. Also banished from France, Du Bosc served a refugee church in Rotterdam. On a final theological note, both Claude and Du Bosc agreed with Daillé that Amyraut's gospel theology was the biblical via media between Arminian sub-orthodoxy and Bezan, ultra-orthodoxy. In short, all these men (and others) were 'legitimate sons of Calvin'.

Eloquent expositor

Regarding Daillé's preaching, Quick writes that 'as for sermons, few ministers have printed more, and which have met with kinder acceptance from the world than his'. Indeed, the warm and experimental Reformed Christianity of Daillé's *Expositions of Philippians* (1643) and *Colossians* (1648) was immensly appreciated on this side of the Channel. Published in the UK by James Nichol (Edinburgh, 1863), the Huguenot preacher's sermons have never failed to instruct and inspire. Daillé's Nichol series editor James Sherman (1796–1862, formerly minister of Castle Street Chapel, Reading and the Surrey Chapel, London) quotes an unnamed 'devoted servant of Christ' who had written on his copy of the 1672 edition, 'This is the most eloquent book in my library'.

In the eighteenth century, Henry Venn, the 'Methodist' Rector of Huddersfield and later of Yelling, Huntingdonshire, wrote to his son John in August, 1784 of the reviving influence of Daillé's sermons: "This last week has been very gloomy, cold, misty weather: we have not had one visitor; but I have enjoyed a feast, in reading M. Daillé on the Colossians. What a judicious writer! What a masterly expositor! The truth, the fulness of Christ, are so set forth by him, as to make my heart glow; and I am the better for what I read." By October, Venn had finished the book: "I have now gone through Daillé on the Colossians, and never was more instructed and entertained."

James Sherman's own commendation of Daillé's sermons is

impressive: 'They are marked by clear interpretation of Scripture—great candour towards other expositors—boldness for the faith—and vigorous attacks on the errors of the papacy, which he exposes with singular skill, and refutes with masculine energy. His sanctified eloquence appears in every page, but especially in his perorations, which for close appeals to the conscience, ardent love to a precious Saviour, earnest exhortations to holy walking with God, and active service for Christ, exceed any which have fallen into the editor's hands...' Somewhat less striking, C. H. Spurgeon's brief remark on Daillé's expositions is not to be ignored: 'Written in a deliciously florid style. Very sweet and evangelical: after the French manner'.

A recent commendation justifies continuing interest in Daillé. Dr Cyril J. Barber writes in the Klock & Klock facsimile edition (1983) of Daillé's *Colossians*: 'In contrast to some puritan works of this period, Daillé adhered more closely to the text of Scripture, expounded each verse fully, and generally leaves his readers astonished at his wisdom and insight'.

It is surely fitting to allow this prince of Huguenot preachers the last word—or shall we say 'words'? The following extracts perfectly illustrate those evangelical virtues for which Daillé's sermons were famous. We begin with his exaltation of his Saviour. Indeed, no one gloried in the person of our Lord Jesus Christ more than Jean Daillé:

Champion for Christ

Jesus, manifested in the flesh, received and treated with so much ignominy and opprobrium upon earth, the stumbling-block of the Jew, the scorn of the Gentile, is, nevertheless, in reality the Lord, the true and eternal God, the Son and the Christ of the Father, the King of the universe, the Father of eternity. Angels shall encompass his throne with profound respect; men, both dead and living, shall all appear before his tribunal, and after having worshipped him and confessed that he is Lord, shall receive from his mouth the sentence either of life or death.

Such are the rights and effects of this great name, which the Father has given to the Son as the price of his obedience. Let us yield ourselves then, dear brethren, in good time to his power. Let us kiss the Son, whom God has given to be our Lord and Master. Let us adore his name; let us bow our knees and our hearts before him. Let us confess that he is Lord. Let us believe it in our heart, and proclaim with our mouth; and if we acknowledge him in this dignity, let us yield him a faithful and constant obedience.

May his will be the only rule, and his glory the sole desire of our lives. Let us leave other men to run after the foolish and perishable objects of their desires, some worshipping one thing, and some another, according to their vain imaginations. As for us, my brethren, may the name of Jesus be our portion; may it be our fear and our dread. Let us have no desire in our minds which does not bow in reverence to him, no interest in our lives which does not yield to his glory. Far from us be the extravagance of those who are ashamed of Jesus Christ and of his gospel. O wretch! are you ashamed of a name which is above every name? Are you ashamed of a name which all the universe adores, and before which the devils and hell tremble? On the contrary, let us make it our greatest glory. May the profession of this name be our dress and our ornament. Let the marks of it be engraven on every part of our life; let us make our children, and all those who are most dear to us, wear its livery (*Sermon on Philippians 2:9–11*).

Living for Christ

For Daillé, in the light of such sublime Christology, there can be only one response to such a glorious Lord and Saviour:

May the Lord Jesus be magnified in your bodies both in life and death. During life, clothe them with the ornaments of the Lord, with chastity, purity, honesty, modesty and humility. May your tongue ever speak His praises, may your eyes ever contemplate His wonders, and your ears ever listen to His teaching; may your feet ever run in His paths, your hands labour in His works; may your persons only be found in those places where [His] great name ... is not ill spoken of (*Sermon on Philippians 1:19–21*).

Roman apostasy

As Sherman correctly remarks, Daillé robustly refuted the claims of the Church of Rome. Indeed, he was not slow to defend the Reformed Faith on the grounds that Roman teaching consisted of post-apostolic novelties:

Whence we may deduce, as we pass on, an invincible proof, both of the truth of the doctrine which we believe, and of the vanity of that which we contest with our adversaries of Rome. For as to what we hold, it is evident that the apostles taught it in all the world, both by word of mouth and by writing, as all the necessary, positive, and affirmative articles of our faith fully appear in the monuments of apostolic preaching; that is, both in the books which they wrote, and in the churches they founded. As for our adversaries, it is no less evident that they can never show that the monarchy or infallibility of their pope, or the adoration of their host, or the service of their images, or the invocation of their saints, or purgatory, or the traffic of their indulgences, or any other of the points which we debate with them, was preached in all the world at the time of the holy apostle. Not a single trace of them can be found in any of the books or memorials remaining of that age, or of a long time beyond it; only a man may perceive them, some ages after, growing up, one in one place and another in another, at various times and in different regions; an evident sign that they are not parts of the gospel of Jesus Christ, which was fully preached in all the world in St Paul's lifetime, but the inventions and traditions of men that have arrived since (*Sermon on Colossians 1:6–8*).

Justification by faith

Needless to say, Daillé—like Luther, Calvin and all the reformers—gloried in the atoning, substitutionary death of our Lord Jesus Christ as the only foundation of the sinner's justification and salvation before God. How are sinners counted righteous before God?

All in virtue of that obedience which Jesus rendered to the Father on the cross, where he was made sin and a curse for us, his agonies being imputed to us as though we had suffered them'. Truly, God communicates the righteousness of faith 'in imputing to the believer the obedience of the Mediator, regarding him with a favourable eye when thus clothed as it were with Jesus, and crowning him with all the benefits he purchased by his death upon the cross (*Sermon on Philippians 3:9–11*).

Faith and good works

As in the sixteenth century, Daillé and his brethren of the seventeenth had to rebut Rome's accusations that the Reformed doctrine of justification produced moral laxity:

And in this our day, is not our doctrine misunderstood and calumniated in the same way? Do they not say, since you are justified by faith alone, what inducement have you to perform good works? But, O ye adversaries it is to perform good works that I am justified. This divine righteousness of Christ has been communicated to me, in order that I may be transformed into his image; that I may know the power of his resurrection, and that I may be like him, a new creature; that I may love God, not to lay him under obligation to me, (far, far from my soul such a preposterous notion) but to acquit myself in a small degree of the immense debt I owe him. I love him because he has loved me, because God is love, and because he has sent his Son Jesus to die and rise again for me. Will my obedience be less acceptable to him because I think not of merit in rendering it? Will he reject it because the cross and resurrection of Christ inspires it, and not an intention of deserving a reward? ... Why may I not serve God here on earth in the same manner as I hope to serve him hereafter in heaven, with a pure, a free, and truly filial affection? And such affection, far from presuming to acquire any right or reward from so good and so merciful a Father, must after all its efforts remain dissatisfied with itself, and be content to ascribe all it has been able to do to his free grace alone (*Sermon on Philippians 3:9–11*).

Electing love

As one might expect, Daillé traces our salvation by 'free grace alone' back to sovereign, divine election. Christians 'have the honour to be elected of God, the saints, and the beloved of God'. Accordingly,

> The election of God is the choice which he makes, according to his good pleasure, of certain persons, to call them to the knowledge of himself, and the glory of his salvation. And this term, election, signifies sometimes the resolution he has taken in his eternal counsel to choose and call them, which Scripture elsewhere calls the determinate purpose of God, Eph. 1:11 (*Sermon on Colossians 3:12–13*).

The universal offer

As with Calvin, Amyraut *and* the Canons of Dordt, Daillé is not paralysed by the decree of God into suppressing the free offer of the gospel. He resists the scholastic rationalism of the day in not explaining away the universality of the gospel:

> [Christ] is the propitiation for the sins of the whole world', 1 John 2:2, and the worth of his sacrifice so great that it abundantly suffices

to expiate all the crimes of the universe; and although the salvation obtained by him is really offered, and by his will, unto all men yet none actually enjoy it but those that enter into his communion by faith, and are by that means in him, as that clause of his covenant expressly imports, 'God so loved the world, that he gave his only begotten Son, that whosoever believeth in him should not perish, but have everlasting life,' John 3:16 (*Sermon on Colossians 1:14*).

Holiness and assurance

For Daillé, the doctrine and experience of the gospel produces holiness and purity of life. It also produces joy and assurance in the believer's heart, notwithstanding the trials of this life:

> Rejoice, then, believing souls, in your Divine Redeemer. Drown every care in these sweet reflections:...In this case you will never [lack] a subject of rejoicing. For you perceive the apostle commands you to be always joyful: "Rejoice in the Lord always;" and, as if he were immediately in a transport of joy himself, he adds, "and again I say rejoice." Listen not to the flesh, which now whispers in your ear that this may be very well for the day of prosperity; but that in the season of affliction, when bending beneath the cross, when sickness weakens, when losses afflict, or when persecution presses hard, it would then be out of season then to say "Rejoice." The flesh, brethren, comprehends not this mystery; it surpasses its sense and understanding. The joy of the Lord is unlike that of the world, which the vapours of the earth extinguish, which is easily overturned by the casualties of life; the joy of Christ is eternal; it maintains itself against everything; nothing can extinguish it; it lives even in the furnace of affliction; and triumphs over death itself (*Sermon on Philippians 4:4–7*).

Suffering

Daillé knew how to be pastorally practical, not least where sickness and suffering were concerned:

> Never let the illnesses with which God visits us either make us doubt his love or our election. He has truly promised us in this world his friendship, his peace, the joy of his Spirit, and the assistance of his Christ, and in another immortality. But he nowhere promises that we shall be exempted from the evils and miseries of the present life. He declares to us on the contrary, that we shall be more subject to them than others. Let us then receive these strokes from his hand

with patience and gentleness of mind, and instead of murmuring or hardening ourselves under the rod, let us profit by it as a salutary correction and an honourable trial, learning from it the vanity of this life, and of all the good that it possesses, thinking rightly of the infirmity of our nature, and of death, which will assuredly destroy it, to withdraw our affections from earth, to renounce vice and its lusts, and to aspire only after a blessed immortality, the end and prize of our holy calling. And as to your life, if it is useful, either to the church or to your families, I do not forbid that you desire it; I simply wish that you would ask it from God, and expect it from his mercy alone, who brings to the tomb, and lifts you from it, when he will; and that, when you have recovered your health, you would ascribe to his goodness all the glory of your cure, devoutly consecrating to his service all the fruits of a life which you only hold from his grace (*Sermon on Philippians 2:25–30*).

It is impossible to do justice to Daillé's preaching in a few extracts. Suffice to say that on every branch of doctrinal, experiental and practical Christianity, his expository skills justify the reputation he acquired in his lifetime. The two volumes of published sermons in English invite one to hope that the many French volumes deposited in Geneva might one day also appear in English. We conclude with Daillé's eloquent encouragement to the pilgrim people of God:

Perseverence and victory

We have a part in the heritage of the saints. The kingdom of the beloved Son of God has been given us. O great and magnificent portion! Let the world boast of and adore its gold, its honours, and its delights, as much as it pleases; we have that better part, which is sufficient to make us eternally happy, though we should be deprived of all other things. Christian, if the world were to bereave you of what you have within its jurisdiction, consider, it cannot take from you the inheritance of the saints. If it denies you its leeks, and onions, and flesh-pots, it cannot debar you from that Divine light which shines on you, and which, in spite of all its attempts, will conduct you to your blissful Canaan. If it takes from you its honours, should it drive you even out of its dominions, it will not be able to wrest from you the kingdom of the Son of God, nor the dignity and glory you possess in it. This is not a corruptible kingdom; it is not like those of the earth, that are subject to a thousand and a thousand dishonours, miseries, and mutations. It is an immortal kingdom, firmer than the heavens; so abundant in glory and in goodness, that it changes all those who partake of it into kings and priests. Faithful brethren, let us be contented with so advantageous a portion. Let us enjoy it for the present by a lively and established hope, meekly bearing the inconveniences of this brief journey we are taking to attain it, and patiently expect that blessed day, when our heavenly Father, having finished the work of his grace, will elevate us all into his glory, and put on our heads the crowns of life and immortality, which he has promised us in the eternal communion of his well-beloved Son. To whom, with the Father and the Holy Spirit, the true and only God, blessed for ever, be all honour and praise, for ever and ever. Amen (*Sermon on Colossians 1:12–13*).

Further reading:

Armstrong, B. G., *Calvinism and the Amyraut Heresy: Protestant Scholasticism and Humanism in Seventeenth-Century France* (Madison: University of Wisconsin Press, 1969)

Baird, H. M., *The Huguenots and the Revocation of the Edict of Nantes*, 2 vols (London: Hodder & Stoughton, 1895).

Bayle, P., *Dictionary Historical and Critical* (London: 1735), (article under 'Daillé').

Benedict, P., *The Faith and Fortunes of France's Huguenots, 1600–85* (Aldershot: Ashgate, 2001)

Clifford, A. C., *Calvinus: Authentic Calvinism, A Clarification* (Norwich: Charenton Reformed Publishing, 1996; 2nd ed. 2007).

Daillé, J., *Exposition of Philippians and Colossians* (Edinburgh: J. Nichol, 1863).

Heath, R., *The Reformation in France*, 2 vols (London: The Religious Tract Society, 1886).

Quick, J., *Synodicon in Gallia Reformata* (London: 1692).

——'The Life of Monsr Daillé, Minister of Paris', *Icones Sacrae Gallicanae* (1700), MS on deposit at Dr Williams's Library, London, DWL 6. 38–39 (39).

Van Stam, F. P., *The Controversy over the Theology of Saumur, 1635–1650* (Amsterdam & Maarssen: APA—Holland University Press, 1988).

4

Fulchran Rey

Besides such famous French Reformed martyrs as Claude Brousson (1647–98), there were many others who deserve our attention. For dedicated and sacrificial service in the cause of Christ, young Fulchran Rey (1661–86) is worthy of special consideration. Though considerably younger than Brousson by over a decade, Rey was martyred more than a decade before his older brother in Christ. In fact, his life is the penultimate biography in John Quick's French *Icones*. The Englishman's account, based on borrowed documents, records an amazing individual who, by the grace of God, triumphed over the greatest hostility ever faced by the Reformed churches of France. For the brevity and brilliance of his ministry, perhaps no pastor shone more brightly for Christ than Fulchran Rey.

A martyr is born

Quick's biography reveals some astonishing pre-natal facts about Rey's life:

> M. Rey was born of godly parents at Nîmes the capital city of Lower Languedoc about the year of our Lord, 1661. Before he came unto this mortal world God signified unto his mother what should befall her child, what should be his calling, and what his life and death. For in the deep slumbers of the night she had this dream, that an eagle upon the wing with two quills in his beak pitched just by her. And immediately she heard one speaking to her, "Mark well what thou seest. For one of those quills in the eagle's bill signifieth, that the child, which is now in thy womb shall preach the everlasting Gospel; and that other quill informs thee, that this child of thine shall seal with his blood that very Gospel which he shall preach unto the world."

Being good Reformed believers, Rey's parents gave little credence

to religious dreams. They would certainly never view them as
'revelations' from God. However, after sharing her dream with
her husband, he could not dismiss it easily. He concluded that 'this
dream is not the product of an idle fancy, but hath something of
great importance in it':

> For those two quills plucked out of their natural places, and the
> voice which spake unto her intimated to them, as they conceived,
> God's purposes concerning this their unborn son, that he should be as
> a Nazarite separated from his brethren, and that he should participate
> of the rapidity of the eagle, with a quick and incredible swift motion
> preach the everlasting Gospel. And that the other quill plucked also out
> of its proper place signified to them, that this very son of theirs should
> be snatched violently out of this world, after that he had finished his
> ministry and testimony, and as the last act of his life should seal the
> truth of the blessed Gospel with his purest heart blood.

A pastor is prepared

Soon after their son's birth, 'the dream recurred again unto their
minds and memory: whereupon they resolved to breed him up
in good learning'. Careful to provide him with a good and godly
education, Fuchran's parents ensured for him sound tuition in
languages, philosophy and theology. Although Quick doesn't
mention the academic institution in which their son studied, it
was possibly the Reformed academy of Montpellier, since the
one in Nîmes had been suppressed as early as 1664. Making great
progress in both general academic study and special pastoral studies,
young Fulchran impressed all who witnessed his development.
According to Quick,

> The professors in the academies, the ancient pastors of the churches,
> and persons of judgement in those congregations where he preached
> upon trial, approved and applauded his excellent gifts of knowledge
> and utterance, and the singular fervour of his spirit in prayers, by
> which he inflamed the most frozen, and animated the most slothful
> unto devotion in that holy duty.

However, as explained by Quick, the iniquitous Revocation of
the Edict of Nantes (1685) now taking effect, the young man's
ecclesiastical recognition was frustrated by the dismemberment of
the Reformed synodical structures:

> Such was the iniquity of the times, and the tyrannical power of their malignant adversaries the Papists, that the Sessions of their Synods both National and Provincial were quite suppressed, the liberty of holding those Assemblies was utterly taken away from the Protestants. The Edict of Nantes, and all other Edicts made in their favour were abolished, and most violent persecution against them raged throughout the whole kingdom, their temples were demolished, and all meetings for religious worship were upon the several penalties interdicted.

Despite the difficulties he faced, Fulchran Rey was determined to fulfil his calling to the ministry:

> But all these terrible difficulties had not sufficient power to take him off from that work unto which he was predestinated by God, and for the performance of which he had such a loud internal vocation. The Holy Spirit and his own conscience supplying the present defects of synodical authority, he entered in these times of confusion and desolation upon the functions of the ministry, and obeyed that call, which he had now received from heaven, and resolved, the necessity and distresses of the Church being so very great and urgent, not at all to leave France, especially, because the pastors being exiled, their flocks were all destitute, and lay open to the devouring jaws of those ravenous wolves the Romish priests and Jesuits. He therefore contrived with himself how he might tarry behind, and preach the Gospel unto his friends and acquaintance, that so he might succour the feeble minded, and confirm those who were yet standing.

Apathy and encouragement

Concerned to encourage the lapsed Reformed faithful in southern France, Rey encountered little enthusiasm among them for his ministry. At Montauban, Millhau, St Affrique and Pont de Camarès, it was the same story. Persecution and oppression had robbed so many believers of their piety. Fear and Louis XIV's 'political correctness' had seduced the Reformed back to the Roman mass. Even among his relatives, Fulchran found that they had 'been charmed with the enchantments of seducers' and 'were become as the deaf adder, which stopped her ear at the voice of this divine messenger'. As Quick relates, deeply distressed at the scale of the apostasy Rey encountered, he found succour in Psalm 142, whose

words and haunting melody in the Genevan Psalter ministered
perfectly to his soul:

> With all my voice to God I cry;
> I call upon the LORD most high.
> Before His face my grief I show
> And tell my trouble and my woe.
>
> To Thee I pour out my complaint,
> For I am weak, my spirit faint.
> When cares with gloom encompass me,
> The path I take is known to Thee.

> (*Book of Praise: Anglo-Genevan Psalter*)

However, as Rey was about to discover, not all had 'bowed the
knee to Baal'. The Lord's servant remained prayerful and hopeful,
and not in vain, as we discover from Quick's vivid narrative:

And the good providence of God answered his every prayers and
expectations. For he was led he knew not how unto two gentlemen,
whom he acquainted with his present condition. They receiving
the narrative of his troubles from his own mouth bade him be of
good cheer, for they would stand between him and all dangers, and
supply him with all necessaries for the support of his life These
gentlemen were both godly Protestants, and who had took up the
cross and suffered much tribulation for the sake of the Gospel, and
who to preserve their liberties, consciences, and lives were forced
to run from one place unto another, sheltering themselves here and
there among their friends that would lodge and entertain them.
And this is remarkable that at this very time they were seeking for a
minister to instruct and comfort them, to corroborate and confirm
their desponding spirits in this hour of temptation of the power of
darkness, when M. Rey accosted them. They received him into their
company most gladly, and the rather that they might be edified with
his holy counsels and discourses, and resolved that they would follow
him wherever he went to preach the Gospel. And accordingly they
went with him unto several houses in the country, into woods, and
mountains, where they had many golden opportunities of hearing the
word. And the word of God was more precious than gold, because
there was no open vision, and that they got this food for their souls
with the peril of their lives. At these meetings God blessed him with
much success, for he preached many sermons, and prayed frequently,
and was at work night and day in fortifying the brethren.

After ministering in this manner for a considerable time, Fulchran desired to visit his parents in Nîmes. Passing through Montpellier, he met several pastors who were trying to get passports to leave France, being banished by the King if they refused to return to Rome. Lengthy conversations with them made Fulchran determined not to flee. Eventually arriving at home, he ministered at gatherings of the Reformed in the vicinity of Nîmes. However, the popularity and effectiveness of his preaching began to arouse suspicion. Enemies of the Truth were busy in pursuing the faithful servants of Christ. 'Many of those pious souls were apprehended', says Quick, 'and cast into loathsome prisons and dungeons, others condemned unto the galleys, and the rest were all dissipated and scattered into corners. Yet this was observable, that among those whom they had imprisoned they could not by any threats or flatteries, frights or promises, get so much as one person to turn informer, and to be an accuser of his brethren'.

An enemy within

As for Rey's activities, they continued unhindered until he was betrayed by a companion. Quick appropriately described the situation:

> M. Rey indeed was betrayed to the men in power by one whose name was Andoyer, a most imprudent dissembler, another perfidious Judas, who professing a particular affection for him, and care of him, did not yet play the traitor, impeaching him, and endeavoured most villainously to betray him. No wonder that he was false unto his friend, who had been so unto his God. This wretch though an apostate yet counterfeited the Reformed Christian to the life, and under this disguise followed M. Rey in all his removes, and informed the civil magistrates where, when, and how he might be taken. But his hour being not yet come, he escaped their gins and traps, and saved himself from their mischievous hands by a speedy flight.

Rey moved on to Castres, where his ministry was warmly received. However, the 'tempest of persecution' was increasing significantly. Returning to Nîmes, 'he hid himself among the faithful in the country villages':

> Here he spent most of his time in writing letters unto the Protestants

that were in prison for the Gospel's sake, and yet of a good conscience; not for having been thieves or murderers, but only for their fidelity unto the Lord Jesus, whose servants they were, as also that they would not be like weathercocks, to change their religion with every turn of the times, and to put off the livery of Christ, and of their holy profession. He encouraged them to undergo patiently their sore trials, and to support courageously under the heavy pressure of their chains; assuring them that those very chains were very glorious in the sight of God, saints, and angels, because they were borne by them for the interest of Jesus Christ.

A call from the Cévennes

Receiving a call from the distressed Protestants in the Cévennes, Fulchran Rey responded with fervent pastoral compassion. However, he was increasingly aware of the dangers ahead. Anxious to prepare his parents (although his mother had possibly died) for every eventuality, he wrote thus to his father:

"Most dear and Honoured Father,

When as Abraham went up unto mount Moriah in obedience to that express command, which he had received from God to offer up in sacrifice his beloved son Isaac, he did not consult with flesh and blood, but proceeded resolutely in that difficult work, and went up into the mount strong in faith, believing that in the mount the Lord would be seen, as in truth He was, man's extremity being God's opportunity. And God accepted of his obedience. It is true the Lord hath not spoken to me face to face as he did unto that great patriarch, but the inspirations and dictates of my conscience tell me that I must be a sacrifice for my God, and that I must be offered up for the service of his Church. I am not infallibly certain whether God will accept of my will for the deed, without exposing me to death, but whatever may come, my will is resigned up unto the divine Will. Not my will, but God's be upon me. In case you should hear that I am taken, I beseech you, sir that you would not repine nor murmur. Brook patiently whatever the Lord shall inflict upon me, it being his own glory, and the enlargement of his Church and kingdom. O! What an happiness would this be unto me, if I might be counted worthy to be numbered with those persons who shall publish his praises, and die in his quarrel."

Undaunted, Rey headed for the Cévennes. His mission was clear. The Reformed people must be encouraged to resist the flesh-pleasing charms of Rome and remain faithful to their God-given heritage. Thus Rey ministered as a true 'son of Calvin'. The trumpet of the Reformation echoed among the mountains of the Cévennes. He declared to the people, writes Quick, 'that that doctrine which they had received was the very Truth of God, that they should love it because of its purity, and keep it most carefully from the men of this world, who like hucksters [aggressive door-to-door salesmen] would blend and mingle it with their corrupt inventions. But they should guard themselves against those lies and impostures, and preserve charily this precious depositum, which God had committed to their trust, and which would in the last day be re-demanded by God at their hands. That it was a treasure of such an immense worth and value that it were better by far to lose all they had in the world than to lose this. That relations, estates, liberties, name, yea, and life itself should not be so dear unto them as the Holy word of God. That this faith, and religious profession of it, and obedience to it was the only direct way to heaven and eternal glory, and that if God called them unto it, they were bound to seal his Truth with their purest and dearest heart blood'.

The cost of discipleship

John Quick provides a specimen of Rey's preaching. Did one ever hear such an eloquent call to costly discipleship? What a rebuke to the cosy and comfortable Christianity so common in the 21st century West from this 17th-century French Reformed pastor in his mid-twenties!

> Yet, yet are the champions of our Lord Jesus, that have fainted in the combats, and are now revived and returned unto the battle, and you courageous combatants, who have stood your ground hitherto stoutly and faithfully, acquit yourselves manfully as good soldiers of Jesus Christ, endure resolutely all the attacks of Satan and his emissaries, bear up against the efforts of that red dragon, and the bloody wounds which you shall receive from the armed troops of his brutish and barbarous dragoons. Be strong in the Lord, and in the power of his might. Put on the whole armour of God, that you may be enabled to resist the assaults and snares of the devil, and that you may not be moved from your steadfastness and duty in those

terrible conflicts you shall have with your merciless enemies. I am
well acquainted, and so shall you also be with the rage and fury
of our adversaries. They are not satisfied with those evils we have
already suffered from them, but they are mustering up worse and
far more grievous against us. They long eagerly to be glutted with
your blood, and to gourmandize upon your goods and substance,
and they will boggle at nothing that they may obtain their ends.
If they block up your passages, that you may not flee, it is on this
design that they may sheath their swords in your bowels, or hang
you upon the gibbets, or burn you at the stake. Stand your ground.
Hold fast your integrity, and be faithful to the death; that you may
not lose your crown; for they are most obstinately bent upon it to
rob you of that guerdon [reward]. Show therefore more constancy
in resisting them than they show fury in your torments.

As Claude Brousson later found, such preaching as this saw
thousands reclaimed for Christ. Wonderful testimonies among the
faithful were the fruit of such preaching. Many, writes Quick, 'in
the midst of all the racks and tortures of incarnate devils' would
'no more falsify their promises, but keep the covenant they had
now renewed so solemnly with God even unto death'.

The road to martyrdom
Not surprisingly, Rey's incessant labours took their toll on his
health. So, after an intense six-week period of mountain ministry,
he withdrew to Anduze for a rest. This did not actually involve
a total break from preaching. However, this relative respite was a
major turning point in his brief ministry. Quick succinctly says that
'it was at that town that God put a stop unto his godly purposes'.
   Quick's vivid and impassioned narrative explains what happened:

   For a certain fellow called Atmeras betrayed him. This Atmeras was
   an inhabitant of Anduze, and who had been his guide and inseparable
   companion up and down the province of Cévennes. The charity of
   this blessed servant of Christ was of the right stamp, it thought none
   ill, was not suspicious, nor did he in the least distrust this treacherous
   villain, who had accompanied him as his bosom friend at all meetings,
   and made him infinite promises of fidelity, insomuch that he deposited
   in his bosom his greatest secrets, and acquainted him with all his places
   of retirement where he was to eat or sleep. Yet did this perfidious
   Judas, this double tongued, and double hearted Ahithophel lift up

the heel against him, and for a little sordid pelf [money], betrayed, sold, and delivered him into the hands of the bloody dragoons, who not in the least forgetting the cruelty of their lord and master, did exercise all kind of barbarity towards him.

The violence that followed demands to be related in Quick's own words:

> They seized on him upon a Saturday night, at a house without the town, as he was deep in study and preparation for the Lord's Day. They had no sooner laid their hands upon him than they clapped him up close prisoner in the guildhall of Anduze, but it was with a most inhuman violence. One of the most inveterate among them took him by the hair of his head, and dragged him along the streets unto the prison. At this inhumane usage, he told the brute that thus treated him, "Friend, remember that God will recompense thee according to thy doings." These words of his were prophetical, and fulfilled upon the spot: for this cruel butcher, having manacled M. Rey's hands with iron cuffs, and locked him up in a dark hole of the prison, being upbraided by one of his comrades that very day for his inhumane carriage towards this his prisoner, he was so transported at these just reproaches, that he draws his sword upon him. The other seeing himself in danger by this enraged aggressor to preserve his own life doth nail him dead upon the ground, the supreme Judge making his fellow trooper the executioner of his just vengeance upon this blasphemer, for he died vomiting out and disgorging whole volleys of curses and blasphemies against God. There is this most remarkable, that with the first blow of his sword he cut off that very hand which had dragged this servant of God along the streets, and with a second blow, he cut that throat wherewith the Majesty of heaven was blasphemed. He died weltering in his own blood a little while after he had received these two wounds. Thus God rewarded him according to his doings, as this holy man of God had spoken. After he had used violence, the very same violence was repaid him, and after he had dealt cruelly with the innocent, the Lord causeth his own companion in arms to deal cruelly with him; the same measure that he had meted out unto his better, was by his own neighbour meted out again unto him, but the measure was pressed down, heaped up, and running over. O! Lord, Thou art just and right in all Thy judgements, and Thy counsels of old are faithfulness and truth.

All-sufficient grace

Locked in the Anduze prison, chained and guarded by six dragoons, and denied visitors, Fulchran Rey 'was now conformable unto his great Lord, our blessed Saviour, even abandoned of all his disciples and followers. But he was strengthened from above with strength in his soul, and was prepared for all events, and this very providence found him ready to suffer the worst and utmost without murmuring or repining'.

Visited by the local judge, Rey was subjected to several interrogations in his cell. Of course, all his pastoral activities were forbidden by the Revocation of the Edict of Nantes. When asked why he persisted in these proscribed pursuits, his answer was predictable. This pastor of souls answered, that 'it was to comfort their hearts in these times of desolation, to confirm them in the fear of God, and to bring them to repentance for all their sins'. Getting nowhere with his prisoner, the judge 'delivered him up to thirty dragoons' who were to transfer him to Alès.

By now, news of Rey's situation was spreading. Quick says that 'When he was brought out of the prison of Anduze, several women followed him sighing and weeping, and pouring out a torrent of tears after him. When M. Rey saw them in that posture, he turned about unto them and said, "Why weep you? Why do you afflict your souls for me? Weep not for me, but for yourselves, and for your sins, that you may find grace, and obtain mercy at the hands of God. For this your tears are needful, and for this you should sigh very continually."

Arriving at Alès, the prisoner was confined to a cell and again interrogated by M. Le Fevre the Lieutenant Criminal of Nîmes. The same questions produced the same answers as before. Not in the least intimidated, Rey was visited by 'monks of several orders, who employed their utmost effort and skill to make him change his religion'. His steadfastness made a deep impression on the monks:

> And those discourses which he had with them about his religion, and his duty of preaching, and immoveable purpose to persevere unto the last in his faith, though he were to die for it, wrought such impressions upon their hearts, that when they left him, and came forth into the street they could not forbear weeping a shower of tears, and protested, that they never heard any man speak as this

young man did, nor to give an account of his faith and hope in such an excellent and marvellous manner as he had done.

The authorities fearing the power of his testimony, the prisoner was now guarded more strictly then ever, and with heavier chains. Quick adds that 'they appointed such persons to bring him meat, of whose fidelity and severity they were well assured, and the pretext that they had to cover this their cruelty, was lest someone or other should poison him'.

Triumph in tribulation

By now, Fulchran Rey's fate was a foregone conclusion. A martyr's death was beckoning. Replete with amazing testimony and tenderness, the God-given fortitude of Christ's servant is remarkably narrated by Quick:

> When he was brought out of the prison of Alès a multitude of persons of both sexes, and of all qualities came from all parts of the town to see him before his departure. They were all in tears, and cast their eyes full of pity and compassion upon him, and offered up unto God thousands of prayers for God's blessings upon him. M. Rey also for his part looked towards them with much love and tender affection, and gave them all his blessing, exhorting them all most earnestly to beg pardon of God for their grievous sins, and to do as St Peter did, to rise speedily after their great fall, and to mourn bitterly for their heinous disloyalty and apostasy from the Truth. All the time that he was at Alès, and all along the way after he was out of prison he was baited by the criminal judge, and importunately urged to turn from the Truth, assuring him with many golden promises, and a multitude of repeated asseverations, that if he embraced this his counsel, there should be no hurt done unto him. But he returned him this answer, "Why, Sir, do you tempt me to change my religion, who am fully persuaded in my conscience of its eternal verity, and incomparable purity? I would rather die a thousand times, if it were possible, than so much as once to forsake it. I beseech you, Sir, never speak a word more to me about it." And then added, "I beg one favour of you, which I pray grant me, for 'tis that only one which I shall ever ask of you". "And what is that" said the judge? If I can do it for you I will." "Well then," said M. Rey, "my request is this, that you will not suffer neither my father, nor any of my kinsfolk to visit me, when I shall be in the prison of Nîmes whither you are carrying me". And this he did, that neither he nor they might be

melted at the mutual sight of one another. For nature would show itself in its proper colours, and he was unwilling to be exposed to the temptation of hearing their cries, he having already taken his last leave of, and given his final farewell to them. And in conclusion he entreated the judge to notify unto his father, and his near relations, that he entirely resigned himself to the will of God, so that the most cruel torments, nor the most cruel death, did in the least trouble him.

Faithful unto death

Imprisoned again on arrival at Nîmes, monks alone were permitted to visit the prisoner. Doing their utmost to make Rey renounce the Reformed Faith, all their efforts proved futile. Says Quick:

> But they did not find a reed in him, but a rock. The blast of their arguments was like waves, which dashing against the rock were all dashed to pieces, they had no power in the least over Him. He told them, that he had cast the die long ago, and was invincibly fixed in his resolution to suffer all things for the glory of God and His Truth, which he had preached and defended. The monks were astonished at his constancy, at his presence of mind, the great tranquillity of his soul, and the serenity of his countenance, when he thus answered them, and confessed ingeniously to their acquaintance in the city, that they could gain nothing upon him, whatever fair promises they made unto him.

Taken from the prison during the night, the appointed place of Rey's execution was Beaucaire, a small town on the banks of the Rhône, about 20 km east of Nîmes. Confined to a house, again, only monks and priests were allowed to see and confer with him. Again, all their endeavours to convert the Reformed pastor were in vain. Quick reveals the frustrations of the Pope's men:

> And whole droves of these monkish animals did continually like so many infernal spirits haunt him. But their arguments were so feeble that they could never work upon his heart. They found him always ready to give a reason for the hope to them that asked it of him, and that he was resolved to suffer all things rather than to forgo his religion and his God, and that He preferred death in this cause to life. This they did not keep as a secret, but told the whole world of it, that it was in vain to deal with this young man, he would never turn Papist, never become a Roman Catholic.

The Intendant of the Province—the infamous Bâsville—had no

more success. Tempting the prisoner with every kind of worldly inducement only revealed Rey's devotion to Christ more strongly:

> "My Lord, I do not love the world, nor the things of this world. I count all those advantageous offers, which you make me, as so much dung, dross, and dog's meat. I trample them all under my feet. All these things, yea, and life itself is not dear unto me, provided I may but gain Christ. Whatever kind of death I may be condemned unto, and must suffer for Jesus Christ, I shall count too great an honour for me. I shall be too happy to die in his quarrel. Death will be unto me unspeakable gain."

Christ's prisoner was aware of glorious precedent in his situation. For Quick adds that 'As he thus used the words of Saint Paul, so did he the words of Polycarp, that famous Bishop of Smyrna, when the Proconsul propounded the like terms unto Him, "Sir," said he, "never advise me to forsake that good Master whom I serve. He never did me but good since I was his Servant, and shall I leave him now? No, I shall never do it. It is in vain to solicit me to abandon Him; whatever death I may suffer, I will never leave him nor forsake him"'.

The clearly-disturbed Intendant tried a final, more formal attempt to make the Reformed pastor recant. Quick's graphic account must not be spoiled by abbreviation. Again, the testimony of another famous martyr aided the prisoner in his hour of need:

> Having gained nothing, and finding it impossible for him to gain anything upon him in private, brought him to the bar, and caused him to sit down on the little footstool before him. Where being sat he bespake him in these words, being much affected with his last discourse. "M. Rey, you have yet time to save yourself if you will." "Yea, My Lord," said he, "and this time will I employ it in working out my salvation." The Intendant taking the word out of his mouth, tells him, "M. Rey, you have but one-way to save your life, you must change your religion or die. My Lord, said he, I must then change, I am very well pleased, 'tis to leave this wretched world for the kingdom of heaven, for an happy life in eternity. I long for it; I shall speedily enjoy it." The Intendant replied, "Be not afraid, I will make good my promise to you, your life shall be saved." "But," said M. Rey, "never feed me with the promises of this life, I am wholly weaned from it, I have no longer any hopes for this world, mine are for a better world. I wait for something else. Death will be far

better to me than life;" (subjoining those words of the renowned
martyr at Constance [Jan Hus]), "Do not think to terrify me with
death; had I feared it I had never come unto this place. God who
hath been so gracious to me as to give me the knowledge of the
true religion, even he will enable me to die for it. Talk no more
to me of the good things of this world, I have no relish of them, I
am disgusted with them. I would not for all the treasures of earth
forfeit those in heaven."

Obedient to Christ

Formally charging the accused that Rey's pastoral activities were
'contrary to the King's will', the Intendent received a bold reply:
"But they are not contrary to the will of the King of Kings who
hath commanded them, and 'tis most just and reasonable to obey
God than man." Yet, as Quick makes clear, the pastor's boldness
was not insolent:

> Unto all demands that were made him, he answered with the
> same tone of voice, with much respect, sweetness, and moderation,
> giving evident marks of the entire resignation of his will unto God,
> demonstrating by all his discourses, and gestures, that the Holy
> Spirit of God was abundantly poured out upon him, and that he had
> received extraordinary assistance from heaven in these and all other
> his conflicts. Which also He manifested again when they did afresh
> assault him, soliciting him to consider seriously of his condition.
> Whereunto he thus returned, "I am not now to consider what I have
> to do. I cast up the costs of my holy profession long since what it
> would stand me; I have judiciously and deliberately made my choice.
> I am resolved to take up my cross, and to follow my Lord wherever
> he will have me go. This is no time of treating or bargaining for
> religion. If my God hath so appointed, I am willing and prepared
> for death. Whatever terms and promises may be made me; they shall
> never be able to remove me, nor to take me off from yielding that
> duty to my God, which I owe Him."

If this godly testimony in the face of cruel persecution was
wonderful enough, Fulchran Rey's witness was about to become
even more wonderful:

> After this discourse was finished, they proceeded unto judgment,
> and the sentence pronounced upon him was, that he should be hanged
> by the neck upon a gallows till he were dead; and that before he was
> executed, he should be put upon the rack, that by the tortures of it

he might be forced to make a full confession. He heard this sentence without any change of countenance, or any discomposure of spirit. He never trembled or grew pale upon it. All that he said was this, "You treat me more favourably than the Jews did our Saviour, and you condemn me to a very easy death. I expected to be either broken to pieces upon the wheel, or to be burnt alive at the stake." And then, lifting up his eyes to heaven, "I Thank Thee," said he, "O Lord of heaven and earth for all Thy benefits bestowed upon me. I thank Thee that Thou thinkest me worthy to suffer for thy Gospel, and to die for thee. I thank Thee for this mercy that thou callest me out to suffer such an easy death, where as Thou hadst prepared my soul to suffer the worst, the most cruel death for Thy sake."

According to our biographer's account, it cannot be denied that extraordinary heavenly aid was being granted to God's dear suffering servant:

Having finished this short prayer, they fastened him to the rack. But although they tortured him most horribly, he was a sheep before his shearer that openeth not his mouth. He made no complaints, but suffered the torments with wonderful patience; and when he was interrogated by those that racked him, he only returned this answer, "I have told you all, I can tell you no more." When his judges could not extort any other confession from him than this, they ordered him to be taken off the rack. And being let down, he cast his eyes upon them saying, "You have, my Lords, inflicted as you intended a very sore punishment upon me; but blessed be God, I have felt little pain. I believe you have suffered more than myself. I protest unto you that when I was most distended and tormented by you, I felt very little anguish."

More triumphant grace

Is it possible that this Huguenot hero could take much more of this? Evidently yes, as the record continues:

The grace of God was so triumphant in this martyr, that he seemed to have been divested of his natural sentiments, and to have none other in him but those of divine grace. That he might be in a condition to endure the last combat, upon which he was now entering, and to recover some strength, they invited him to dine. He did not refuse this motion, but complied with their desires, and ate something of what was prepared for him. "Sirs, others eat that they may live, but I that I may die. This is the last repast that I shall make in this

world. I am invited this evening to sit down at the banquet of wine
in heaven. The holy angels will conduct me thither; those glorious
spirits will carry me upon their officious wings into Abraham's
bosom, where I shall participate together with them of the joys and
delights of paradise."

The glory of eternity was opening up before our hero. 'From this
moment' says Quick, 'he was wholly taken up in religious transports
and meditations, he gave himself to prayers and praises'. Indeed:

> He sang with a sweet and clear voice several portions of David's
> Psalms. The fervour of his devotion ravished those that heard and
> observed him, and pierced their hearts to the very quick. The monks
> once more assault him, but his answers to them were so sinewy and
> substantial, that they were struck quite dumb, and departed from him
> without being able to reply one word; yea they were forced with a
> torrent of tears to lament his disastrous and untimely end.

Brought from prison to the place of execution, still the monks
persisted in offering the martyr their comforts. Expressing a holy
annoyance, Rey testified to something superior:

> "I have no need of your company and consolations. I have a far
> better Comforter than you, even one who is more faithful to me. It
> will be ever with me, and it is now in my soul." The monks being
> importunate with him to bear him company, "No," said he, "away
> from me. There is a company of holy angels round about me, and
> these assure me that they will be with me to the very last gasp."

A ladder up to heaven

Walking along the streets in a steady pace, the 'march to the
scaffold' could not have been a more triumphant and touching
spectacle. He strode forward

> …with a contented spirit visible in his countenance, and with that
> assurance as if he were rather going to a feast than to be executed.
> Perceiving some Protestants in the way, he saluted them, and they
> not being able to return the same civility unto him because of their
> great grief and briny tears that gushed out abundantly from their
> eyes, he said unto them, "Why do you weep for me? Weep only
> for yourselves. I shall presently have an end put unto all my sorrows
> and sufferings, and shall be far enough from this vale of tears. I am
> going, but shall leave you behind me. Arise my Brethren you who

are fallen, rise up again, and repent you of your great sin in falling from the Truth, and God will be merciful unto you."

Still the monks harassed our hero. The reward for their irritating efforts was unambiguous: "You are," said the martyr, "most troublesome comforters. I have no business for you, nor do I need any of your assistances." The presence of Christ was even more evident as the place of execution came into view:

> As he passed out through the gate of Beaucaire, he had sight of the gallows, which was set up for him: and no sooner had he got sight of it, but that he felt new transports of courage and piety, which made him cry out, "Courage! Courage! This is the place which I have long since expected, and which God hath Himself prepared for me. How much doth the sight of this place please me! I see the heavens wide open to receive me, and the holy angels, who do now attend me, ready to carry me up thither."

Despite being forbidden to sing a psalm aloud, nothing could quench Fulchran Rey's joyful anticipation of heaven:

> He drew nigh unto the ladder without any fear, and cried out, "O what a mercy will this ladder be unto my soul! I am now one degree nearer my last end; but a few steps more and I shall be in Heaven." At the foot of the gallows he kneeled down and prayed, then he went up around it joyfully, as one who longed earnestly to be at home in his Father's bosom. He spied the monks come up after him, and not being able to thrust them down with his hands, he spake to them, "I pray you go down. I have told you already, that I have no need of your assistance. I receive helps enough from my God to dispatch the last work of my life, and to finish my course."

We close this scene of victorious suffering with the words of Samuel Smiles:

> When [Rey] reached the upper platform, he was about, before dying, to make public his confession of faith. But the authorities had arranged beforehand that this should be prevented. When he opened his mouth, a roll of military drums muffled his voice. His radiant look and gestures spoke for him. A few minutes more, and he was dead; and when the paleness of death spread over his face, it still bore the reflex of joy and peace in which he had expired. "There is a veritable martyr," said many even of the [Roman] Catholics who were witnesses of his death.

If we only hang our heads in shame and disbelief at the human capacity for wickedness and cruelty, we do the memory of Fulchran Rey an even more shameful injustice. He would have us stand amazed at the wonder of God's almighty and all-sufficient grace!

Further reading:

Baird, H. M., *The Huguenots and the Revocation of the Edict of Nantes,* 2 vols (London: Hodder & Stoughton, 1895).

Benoist, E., *The History of the Edict of Nantes,* 2 vols (London: J. Dunton, 1694).

Book of Praise: Anglo-Genevan Psalter, revised ed. (Winnipeg, Manitoba: Premier Printing, 1987).

Gray, J. G., *The French Huguenots: Anatomy of Courage* (Grand Rapids: Baker Book House, 1981).

Heath, R., *The Reformation in France,* 2 vols (London: Religious Tract Society,1886).

Orna-Ornstein, F., *France: forgotten Mission Field* (Welwyn: European Missionary Fellowship, 1971).

Proceedings of the Huguenot Society of London Vol. 2, 1887–88 (London: 1889).

Quick, J., *Synodicon in Gallia Reformata* (London: 1692)

— 'The Life of Mr Fulchran Rey', *Icones Sacræ Gallicanæ* (1700), MS on deposit at Dr Williams's Library, London, DWL 6, 38–39 (49).

Smiles, S., *The Huguenots in France after the Revocation of the Edict of Nantes* (London: Daldy, Isbister & Co., 1875).

5
Claude Brousson

The 50th and final biography of John Quick's French *Icones* records the amazing testimony of the famous martyr Claude Brousson. Born at Nîmes in 1647, Brousson was trained for the bar, serving eventually as an advocate at Toulouse. He frequently defended Protestants with great eloquence against the ever worsening legal enactments issued against them by the Jesuit-inspired policies of King Louis XIV. His life and freedom threatened by the Roman Catholic authorities, Brousson fled to Lausanne. With their temples demolished and the flocks scattered, the mounting persecutions of Reformed believers following the Revocation of the Edict of Nantes in 1685 filled him with distress. After visiting Berlin and Amsterdam to arouse support for the persecuted—and in the face of antagonism from refugee pastors he had criticized for leaving their flocks, Brousson felt the call of God to return to France, not as a lawyer but as a pastor. Returning to the Cévennes in the summer of 1689, he commenced one of the most courageous and sacrificial ministries in the history of the Christian church. His heart bled with Christ-like compassion for pastorless souls who, under the most diabolical pressures of persecution had, in considerable numbers, abjured their faith.

Apostolic ministry
Living with constant danger, exhaustion, deprivation and the discomforts of cave and forest-dwelling in climatic extremes, Brousson's itinerant ministry to the 'churches of the desert' was phenomenal by apostolic standards. Interrupted by recuperative and support-raising visits to Switzerland, Germany and England,

and a brief pastorate in Holland, Brousson's labours ended during his third and final visit to France which began in August 1697. Leaving his family at the Hague, the fears of his tearful wife were now to be realised. He was betrayed and arrested near Pau in south-western France and imprisoned in the Citadel at Montpellier on 30 October 1698. His execution on 4 November proved a glorious demonstration of the all-sufficient grace of God. After the martyrdom of this remarkable servant of Christ, the Montpellier executioner declared, "I have put to death two hundred convicts, but none have ever made me tremble like M. Brousson."

John Quick's biography of Claude Brousson is noteworthy in several respects, not least because in 1694 a personal meeting took place between author and subject during Brousson's visit to England. Writing in 1700, Quick says of his Huguenot hero:

> I had the honour of his acquaintance and was favoured with a conversation with him in my house [in Bunhill Fields] about seven years ago, when he was in London, which lasted five good hours. The time seemed very short unto me, that I was blessed with such a guest…We spent the time in Christian conference and discourse… Not a vain or idle word dropped from his mouth. He seemed an angel in a human body, who was not content to go to heaven alone, but would carry his friends, countrymen and strangers thither together with him also.

Quick's epic account of Brousson's heroic ministry must rank with the most vivid and inspiring Christian literature ever written. From this little known MS material, the following carefully chosen extracts portray Brousson's personal godliness, pastoral zeal and sacrificial dedication to the cause of Christ in the midst of the most horrific, ruthless and brutal persecution of the period. Despite the most determined opposition, his activities and experiences remain unique examples of the all-sufficient and sustaining grace of the living God.

Zealous pastor

Broussons's pastoral labours probably have no parallel in the seventeenth century. In the English-speaking world, even the work of Richard Baxter is not on the same scale. Furthermore, at a time when English Nonconformity was becoming notorious for doctrinal decay and moribund spirituality, Brousson displayed the zeal of purer times. Fifty years before the Methodist Revival, Brousson's itinerant activities anticipated those of Whitefield and the Wesleys, the Huguenot's being conducted in far more hostile conditions. John Quick continues the story:

> In the Cévennes and Lower Languedoc…there were quartered… several regiments of dragoons who rode up and down night and day to hinder all religious meetings; and yet notwithstanding all their pains, subtlety and malice, they were both very frequent and numerous. Every night there was one or more of these assemblies celebrated for divine service; for ordinarily they met at midnight. M. Brousson the first two years of his ministry held very many of them, at least three or four every week, till by the unseasonableness of the time (which in nature was designed for rest) and the overstraining of his lungs in speaking, he quite broke his health, and contracted such a soreness in his breast, as he could never be rid of it to his dying day.
>
> The desolation of the people of God was deplorable. This grieved his very soul. For they being as sheep without a shepherd were every moment exposed to the fury and malice of those evening wolves and ravening bears, the idolatrous priests of the Romish synagogue who shewed them no mercy, but most insatiably worried and devoured them. When he reposed himself a little while, he was necessitated to range over a wild and spacious country to exercise in other assemblies. Sometimes the meetings were nearer, other times at farther distance, according as they could find a conveniency to be together.

Preaching and Psalm-singing

> Before he could tarry at one place a week, he was necessitated upon times to preach ten, twelve, fifteen and once five and twenty sermons at these meetings in the space of eight days. These were indeed the labours of a true apostle of our Lord. For a fortnight together he hath preached every other night; transporting himself that evening in which he did not preach unto the next place appointed for that service. At ordinary meetings he was obliged to speak three hours, and in those of them that the Lord's Supper was administered, no less than four or four and a half. The most of which time was spent in prayer, because of the doleful calamities of God's poor Zion in France. One thing, though it much comforted him, was yet no mean affliction to him, and a mighty prejudice unto his voice. It was this;

he was necessitated to raise all the psalms, and to guide all the people himself, that they might sing musically. And the tunes of the French Psalms as they are most sweet and melodious, so many of them are of very high and lofty notes, to the true singing of which there is required sound lungs, and a clear strong voice. This made him strain his lungs, and put his voice and breast upon the rack. But he was the servant of God and his Church, and he valued not his health, nor counted his life dear unto him, so that he might serve and save souls, fulfil the ministry unto which he was called, and finish his course with joy.

The mighty power of God

After the sermons were ended, he usually made a plain and familiar discourse, in which he exhorted those who by reason of the violence of temptation, and frailty of human nature had fallen from their holy profession, to repent heartily and enter the bosom of the church unfeignedly, and to renounce all the reigning sins of this present age, and the abominations of unclean Babylon, and to swear allegiance and fidelity unto God, and to keep his commandments diligently for the future. And the Lord crowned this exercise with a rare and wonderful blessing. For I remember in those five hours conversation with him in my house, he told me that in one part only of one of the western provinces of France, no fewer than five thousand persons kneeling down upon the bare ground with streaming tears, deep sighs and heart cutting groans, after such familiar exhortations of his, did most bitterly lament their revolt from our holy religion, and with eyes and hands lifted up to heaven did call God to witness upon their souls that they renounced the Romish faith, worship and discipline, that they would never any more have or hold communion with that idolatrous antichristian synagogue, that they would never bow the knee to Baal more, never go to mass, come what there would of it, and that they would hold fast the profession of their faith, and the true religion through the grace of God without wavering, and persevere immovably in it unto the end. This I say was in only one part of a province. But he had reclaimed some thousands more in other provinces. So mighty was the power and presence of God with him in his ministry. He never baptized infants in the larger but lesser assemblies.

Over and besides these labours in their solemn meetings, M. Brousson spent three hours every day in prayer, the first in the morning, the second at three in the afternoon, the third in the evening, for the comfort of those families where he stopped or lodged, as he travelled from one place unto another, or that took upon them the care of his person, and watched for his preservation, or of the faithful who assisted at these holy exercises. He most usually accompanied these prayers with a most lively exhortation unto those who were present at them. He preached twice every Lord's Day, in the morning and afternoon; besides he repeated his sermons unto such of the faithful, as knowing the place of his retreat, would visit him in the evening.

Writing in the wilderness

Nor did he preach the Gospel by word of mouth but did it also by writing. For in those nights in which there were no assemblies, he sat up transcribing copies of his sermons which he sent abroad among the godly, and the subject matter of which were the most important points of Christianity, such as were of indispensible necessity to be known that we might be saved... All his sermons were written in a becoming plainness, suited to the capacity of his auditors and in the divine style of the Sacred Scripture, in the heavenly language which the Holy Ghost taught the divinely inspired prophets, evangelists and apostles to hand down unto us their infallible oracles, books, gospels and epistles. So that through the grace of God he delivered the celestial doctrine in its natural simplicity, purity and evidence: whereby that poor people were wonderfully edified. These little sermons of his took with them most mightily, and 'twas who could purchase them, especially in those places where there were no assemblies nor ministers. To this purpose he always carried with him a little desk to write upon, and which he placed upon his knees when he wrote, and the godly in the Cévennes and Lower Languedoc called 'the table in the wilderness'. So that when his impaired health, and the infernal rage of his enemies hindered and took him off from preaching in the wilderness meetings, yet God granted him this consolation that by his written sermons he preached louder, and was heard at a farther distance, than if he had uttered them before a particular congregation.

Wise theologian

Claude Brousson's ministry did not involve him to any great extent in the disputes associated with the academy of Saumur some fifty years earlier. Two features of his thinking may be highlighted. *First*, whether or not he possessed an accurate grasp of a viewpoint frequently misunderstood, he was not as suspicious of Amyraldian teaching as others had been. Holding to a 'moderate high orthodox' Calvinism,

Brousson's carefully-qualified reservation about Amyraldian theology is thus distinctly mild. In fact, Amyraut and his supporters would not have felt implicated in the charge Brousson gently makes. Indeed, 'novelty' was a feature of the doctrines Amyraut opposed. Writing to the refugee pastors, Brousson warned against other theological aberrations like Arianism, then beginning to gain currency:

> It is still this same spirit of novelty which gave place among us to the doctrine of universal grace [i. e. Amyraut's teaching]. I believe that in France those who held this doctrine encompassed it within very narrow parameters. But we must be careful, my very honoured brothers, not to open the door to error...

Second, it is clear that Brousson did not confine the covenant of grace to the elect as the English Puritan John Owen did, a view developed with paralysing effect by later hypercalvinists in their denial of the free offer of the Gospel. On this, Brousson could not be clearer:

> It is true that the covenant of grace is beneficial to all men. But that can only mean that it is beneficial to those who repent and believe in the Gospel from any country in the world. That is why the Gospel is preached to all people...It is so that we can be led to love all men without distinction and to do all in our power to prevent them from perishing But that does not mean that God absolutely wants the conversion of all men. For if he wanted to convert every single person he could do it...

Resisting Rome

Equally clearly, Brousson was mainly concerned with the protection of Reformed believers from the onslaught of Rome, as John Quick makes clear:

> M. Brousson also did at several reprises contend by other writings in defense of the truth. These were the results of his spare hours, when against his will he had an extraordinary vacation. These he dispatched unto the court at Versailles. Such was his *Apology for the Project of the Reformed in France*, and for those other Servants of God who preached and assembled to worship God in that forlorne kingdom. But God the most righteous judge as he hardened Pharoah and the heart of the Egyptians his subjects, so did God harden the heart of the French king, of the sycophants his counsellors, and of his sodomitical clergy, so that they would not let the Protestants go free

to serve and worship Him, nor to pay unto the Divine Majesty those homages which are due unto Him from men and angels. Yea the task of bricks hath been since doubled and trebled, as the zealous affection of His poor people augmented to follow him in the wilderness there to adore and hold communion with Him. Hence they turned every stone, and tried all kinds of experiments utterly to destroy those few ministers who laboured to instruct and comfort them.

Over and above those five regiments of dragoons before mentioned maintained and dispersed by the clergy in the Cévennes and Lower Languedoc to keep the good people from worshipping God according to His appointments, there were also several garrisons in those two provinces in the forts of Alès, St Hippolyte and at Nîmes. These made it their incessant business either to seize upon or massacre the poor ministers of the word, but their principal aim was at [François] Vivens and Brousson. So that in the year 1691, an ordinance was published in which they promised 5000 livres to him or them, that should take either of these servants of God alive or dead. Thus had anyone liberty to murder them, and those assassins that should make them away were sure of a rich reward from the Government...

Brutal persecution

Like the English Puritans and the Scottish Covenanters, the French Huguenots also had their episodes of military conflict. Whether or not Christians should ever resort to the sword in the face of persecution and despotism is a question of timeless importance. In an atmosphere of relentless provocation, graphically related by Quick, Brousson's teaching and example possess a unique challenge. Its relevance to current discussion cannot be ignored:

But the faithful in the Cévennes being most cruelly oppressed, as yet they are to this very day [1700], it was impossible but that some persons transported with a blind zeal or by the motions of their natural choler which they could not always master, should break out into intemperate actions or expressions, especially when as they saw their nearest relations murdered before their faces without any legal trial, only for serving God. M. Brousson did not approve of such transports and restrained them to the utmost of his power. But sometimes he had to do with men whose spirits were so embittered by reason of those manifold evils they suffered that they grew stark desperate. They would complain, and they had too just and too much ground to complain, that the Edicts most religiously sworn to them were violated, all Treaties of Pacification rescinded, that the most barbarous hostilities were exercised towards the Reformed, that they were against their consciences compelled to abjure the true religion by which they hoped for salvation. They were cruelly tortured in their bodies, plundered of their goods, racked in their consciences, and all for no crime in the least but this, that they kept the commandments of God and therefore they were as sheep devoted to the slaughter and massacred every day.

Death from the dragoons

In Poitou, in Lower Languedoc, in the Cévennes, [the dragoons] had perpetrated already numberless massacres. And if they had not committed murders enough upon Protestants, they fell foul again upon them. One of the ladies of Belcastell received a deep wound in her head with a cutlass. Many of the faithful were killed at a meeting nigh unto St Germain in the Cévennes and a greater number of them wounded, and divers attempting to save themselves were drowned. This was in June 1686. The July following, a great multitude of them as they were at the worship of God about two leagues from Uzès were most of them slaughtered in the very place. The popish dragoons mingled their blood with their sacrifices. Some of both sexes were taken and hanged up immediately.

Violence in the Vivarais and Le Vigan

In October of the same year, 40 persons more for the same heinous crime in meeting together to call upon God were all of them shot dead at Le Vigan in the Cévennes. In the month of February 1689, no fewer than 300 souls were butchered in the place of meeting which was on another mountain of Vivarais, and they cut the throats of about 50 more in the Vaunage. It was that monster of a man (and surely the African monsters were more humane than he) the Intendant Bâsville that did by express orders enjoin these unheard of murders. His dragoons soaked in blood spared neither sex or age, but slew all, young, old, men, women and sucking children indifferently. When the murderers came and assaulted these innocent lambs, they were all at prayer, upon their knees, with their eyes and hands lifted up to heaven; and in this very posture did they kill them either with their carbines or sabres. Yea many of them did open their own breasts voluntarily to receive the mortal shot or blow from them, rather than they would abjure their religion.

One of these dragoons, a worthy apostle of that old red dragon murdered a poor woman, whose little infant was sucking at her breast; and coming up to her, the poor babe smiling upon him held out its pretty hand to play with him. But instead of playing with it, this devil incarnate stabbeth this poor lamb with his bayonet into the heart, and holding it up, crieth unto his comrade, "See, see", saith he, "how this frog which I have stuck yet sprawleth!" When the Intendant Bâsville was informed of this horrible murder, he takes no notice of it, but only asked the murderer whether the woman had any other children. And he answering yes, "Well", quoth he, " 'tis so much the worse for thee. For one time or other they will avenge their mother's death upon thee…"

Resistance or restraint?

Had these poor Christians the patience of angels, they could hardly have born up without resenting of such barbarous inhumanities. Yea, although they found any of the faithful quiet at home, nor at any of these meetings, if they had not their throats cut, yet they were robbed and spoiled of all their goods, their homes demolished, their families dissipated, and the men, as if they had been the most incorrigible villains in nature were condemned unto the galleys. These violences, these murders and massacres made many very sober persons contrary to their former resolutions to grow impatient.

Now though the injustice and cruelty of these bloody persecutions exceeded all bounds, yet M. Brousson could not approve of [François Vivens' violent retaliation against the dragoons] which proceeded from a mistaken and immoderate zeal. His enemies proclaimed open war against him, and he bade defiance unto them. M. Brousson did frequently represent unto him, that the weapons of our warfare are spiritual, and that he should use none other sword but the sword of the Spirit…that is to say the Gospel shall be preached with a spirit of sweetness and love, and it will be by this means, that God will convert the nations and will perfectly set up His kingdom in the whole world. This very doctrine did M. Brousson oftentimes inculcate unto his brother Vivens and to some other Protestants who were acted by the same spirit of fire, zeal and indignation.

Divine aid

Much of Reformed theology's oft-lamented reputation for sterile orthodoxy has its origins in the seventeenth century. Such cerebralism, so it is argued, justifed the warmth and 'enthusiasm' of the Methodist Revival. According to Quick's account, Brousson was far removed from the Dutch and Anglo-Saxon Reformed stereotype. When clinically accurate theology would have been meagre sustenance indeed, Brousson's experiences of the Holy Spirit reveal a higher dimension. He was favoured with an extraordinary assurance, the details of which invite a comparison with the experiences enjoyed by eighteenth-century Methodists in far less threatening circumstances:

Now although M. Brousson was like unto a pelican in the wilderness and an owl in the desert, and forced to lurk in caves and dens of the earth, yet was he continually pursued by his enemies. Which way soever he turned his head he could see nothing else but death before him, yea that death which was most cruel. For the Government was much more exasperated against him than against all the other servants of God. But he was wonderfully supported by divine grace. A thousand times hath he concluded with himself, "All way of escape faileth, I shall certainly now be taken, I cannot but fall into the hands of these Sauls." Infinite times hath he looked martyrdom in the face, and he hath resigned up his soul to God as if the sentence of death were the very next moment to be executed upon him.

Sometimes the Lord hath dawned in with a beam of hope into his heart, and then he would persuade himself that God would never suffer him to fall into his enemy's hands, that He would never sell nor deliver him up to those cruel oppressors, that thirsted for his blood, and prepared for him the most exquisite and unheard of torments. But a while after, he fell into his old fears, darkness and terrible alarms. Insomuch that it was even with him as with Job and David, he was scared with visions and terrified with dreams. Yet recollecting himself and the carriage of divine providence towards him, he would say unto his soul, "Why art thou cast down O my soul? Why art thou disquieted within me? Hope still in God, who is the light of thy countenance and thy God. My life is in His hands. If He will have me die, 'tis not all the world can hinder it. And if I must die, 'tis better dying in the way of duty than in the neglect of it." Whereupon he went and preached the Gospel in those places where he had promised. And the danger was visible, yet the wisdom and mercy of God safeguarded him. He was in the midst of a burning furnace which was heated against him seven times hotter than usual, but the providence of God did most miraculously preserve him...

All-weather pastor

Now and then M. Brousson might get a soft bed at Nîmes, but his ordinary lodging was in the woods, on the mountains, in dens and caves of the earth. He was royally accommodated when he had sweet fresh straw; at other times he must be contented to lie on a dunghill, or upon fagots, to sleep under a tree, under bushes, in the clefts of rocks, and under ground in holes of the earth. In the summer he was consumed with the burning heat of the sun. In the winter he was almost frozen to death upon the cold mountains of ice and snow, not daring to kindle a fire to warm him for fear the smoke or light thereof should discover him, nor durst he get out of his hiding place to enjoy the comfort of the warm sun lest he should be seen by his enemies and false brethren. Many times hath he been pinched with hunger, wanting food to sustain nature, and was fainting away for want of drink. The fatigues that he has endured have brought him so low that he hath been next door to the grave. Wherefore in all those pictures of him which were scattered up and down the kingdom in city and country, in order to his discovery, he was represented as a man of a sallow countenance, tanned with the sun, exceeding thin, and meagre as a skeleton. Yet did none of these things grieve him when he considered that he suffered them in God's service, for His glory and the consolation of his poor people.

And when this poor people considered the calamities and dangers to which he was incessantly exposed in his labours for the salvation of their souls, and when they also reflected upon the innocency of his life and that grace of God given him to preach His word in its native simplicity and purity, in the evidence and demonstration of the Spirit, he never retired from those holy meetings but that several of them would fall upon his neck, kiss him and wish a thousand blessings upon him. Moreover the Lord led him into His banqueting house, displayed the banner of His love over him, made him taste those joys of the Holy Ghost, which are unspeakably sweet, ravishing and full of glory. But he felt those heavenly consolations in his soul mostly when he was preaching or praying in those holy assemblies or administering the Lord's Supper. Then was he stayed with flagons of new wine of the heavenly kingdom; then was he comforted with the apples of the celestial paradise. He was even sick with the love of God, the glories thereof overflowing his feeble nature. Christ's left hand was under his head and His right hand did embrace him.

The peace of God

It is not hard to imagine that, due to the horrific persecutions of the period, one could easily lose one's sanity. Doubtless some suffered terribly in this respect. Yet, many testified to God's remarkable presence, a reality Brousson rejoiced in, as Quick makes clear:

> He had one experience, yet he believed that it was not his own only, but that other servants of God might sense it as well as himself, that although he was environed with armies of enemies, who coursed up and down continually in search of him, yet no sooner was he got into those holy assemblies and had lifted up his heart to God in prayer or had opened his mouth to sing His praises or to preach His word, but that all his carnal servile fears vanished and his mind was as quiet, serene and calm as if he had been in a land of liberty. And he had this great tranquillity of soul whenever he took pen in hand to write in behalf of the truth, for the advancement of God's kingdom and the consolation of His desolate church. He composed also in the midst of these pressing dangers several pieces which are since published and which he sent to Court for the justifying of that doctrine which he preached. This cannot but be wondered at. But God magnified His own glorious power in the weakness of His instrument…

The spreading revival

> From the year 1692, M. Brousson set up those holy meetings again; but his breast was so very sore that he could only preach but once in seven days. Yet was not the people's zeal allayed during his long indisposition. For that taste they had of the sweet and heavenly comforts of the Holy Ghost, and their fear of losing them, the many copies of his sermons, letters and prayers which he had dispersed among them, which falling into the hands of persons of quality and of estate in the world, it raised up such a flame in their souls after the word of God, that now rich merchants, noble gentlemen, lords and ladies with their families and children, who were formerly lukewarm and indifferent as to religion, were melted into repentance, and frequented constantly and conscientiously these religious meetings. By this means, as two flints clashing together will strike out fire, so the zeal of one Christian fired and inflamed another. Insomuch that the greatest care of Brousson and the other preachers was that their meetings might not be too numerous nor public, lest the faithful should be exposed unto persecution. But the news of these religious assemblies made a very great noise not only in the Cévennes and

Lower Languedoc but in all parts of the kingdom, and the godly were very much edified and confirmed by them.

Courageous martyr

No survey of Brousson's life and ministry, however brief, is complete without his martyrdom at Montpellier on 4 November 1698. Quick's account is well attested and profoundly moving:

My author informs me (who was an eye-witness of his martyrdom) that he carried it like a true Christian, of an invincible spirit, one who triumphed over death. There were near twenty-thousand persons present to see him die, most of the nobles of the city and country, besides abundance of foreigners. He prayed earnestly, with his eyes and hands lifted up to heaven all the way as he was going unto execution, nor did he take notice of any person till he came unto the scaffold, his heart and thoughts being wholly taken up with his approaching change. The mildness and courage with which he ascended up the scaffold is not to be expressed. Though as he passed by them the people wept and groaned, bitterly lamenting the hard fate of a person of such eminent merit and piety, yet you might read the inward calmness of his soul in his smiling looks and cheerful countenance.

He gave his watch unto the Captain of the Count of Broglie's Guards and his cloak to one of the Intendant's messengers who had waited upon him during his imprisonment. Upon the scaffold he made a speech unto the people but no one could be edified by it. For the drummers of the Regiment of Guards did all beat an alarm as soon as he began to speak. M. Brousson having ended with his auditors prepareth himself for death. He putteth off his own clothes to his shirt, yielded both his hands and feet to be fastened to the wheel, and whilst they were tying them up, " 'Tis a comfort to me", said he, "that my death hath some resemblance with that of my Lord." The spokes of the wheels were struck into the rands in form of a St Andrew's cross. Being in this posture they pronounce again his final sentence on him which undoubtedly surprised that vast crowd of auditors, if it did not M. Brousson, for he was thereby ordered to be strangled to death, before he was broken on the wheel. This was an unexpected favour. God doth sometimes mollify the hearts of lions. He would not suffer the bloody papists to let out all their rage and cruelty upon His servant.

Magnanimous grace

The executioner having fastened him, went down the scaffold, and being just under the holy martyr, when he had half strangled him, the [metal bar] brake in his hand, so that M. Brousson came to himself again and fell a praying. The Abbé Camarignain hearing him call upon God, came near unto him [to encourage repentance]. M. Brousson seeing him [but rejecting the suggestion] said, "May God Almighty, sir, reward your great charity towards me, and grant us this mercy, that we may see each other's face in Paradise!" These were the last words that he was heard to speak in this world. When he was dead they immediately brake him upon the wheel. He was very much lamented by the sober Papists themselves. And well they might; for if these things be done in the green tree, what will not be done in the dry? A man asked the executioner how M. Brousson died. "If I durst speak it out", said he, "I could say much, but in short, he died a saint, and sealed the truth which he had preached with his heart's blood." Yea and the Intendant Bâsville confessed that he never heard a man talk so excellently as Brousson did...

When the news of his martyrdom was brought unto Lausanne in Switzerland, M. Merlat, formerly Pastor of the church of Saintes in France, but then minister in that city, preaching upon this sorrowful occasion, declared so many excellent things concerning this martyr, that the whole congregation burst into tears.

Not the end

Doubtless disappointed at his inability to publish the *Icones,* John Quick must have been further distressed by news from France and especially the Cévennes during his last years. In the aftermath of Brousson's death, the tragic failure of the Camisard insurrection (1702–4)—largely fought on François Vivens' principles—must have seemed like the end of the Reformed churches in France. However, as Quick was departing from this world, God was preparing the 'Huguenot Nehemiah'. His name was Antoine Court, born at Villenueve-de-Berg in 1696. In 1715, the very year Louis XIV died, this teenager from the Vivarais was called of God to revive the Reformed Faith in France. Unlike 'le grand monarque', the God of the Calvinists was not dead! The renewed vision, intrepid labours and organizing genius of Antoine Court were to vindicate everything Claude Brousson had lived and died for—but that is for the equally amazing sequel (recounted next) to a truly glorious though sad and violent story, part of which was first told by 'our English Quick'.

Further reading:

Baird, H. M., *The Huguenots and the Revocation of the Edict of Nantes,* 2 vols (London: Hodder & Stoughton, 1895).

Baynes, H. S., *The Evangelist of the Desert: Life of Claude Brousson* (London: 1853).

Clifford, A. C., *Calvinus: authentic Calvinism, a clarification* (Norwich: Charenton Reformed Publishing, 1996, 2nd ed. 2007).

Gray, J. G., *The French Huguenots: Anatomy of Courage* (Grand Rapids: Baker Book House, 1981).

Heath, R., *The Reformation in France* , 2 vols (London: The Religious Tract Society, 1886).

Orna-Ornstein, F., *France: forgotten Mission Field* (Welwyn: European Missionary Fellowship, 1971).

Quick, J., *Synodicon in Gallia Reformata* (London: 1692)

——'The Life of Monsr. Brousson', *Icones Sacrae Gallicanae* (1700), MS on deposit at Dr Williams's Library, London, DWL 6, 38–39 (50).

Smiles, S., *The Huguenots in France after the Revocation of the Edict of Nantes* (London: Daldy, Isbister & Co., 1875).

Utt, W. C. & Strayer, B. E., *The Bellicose Dove: Claude Brousson and Protestant Resistance to Louis XIV* (Brighton, UK/Portland, USA: Sussex Academic Press, 2003)

NOTE: While I do not wish to sound ungrateful for the several references to my small book *Sons of Calvin: Three Huguenot Pastors* (Norwich: Charenton Reformed Publishing, 1999) in this last item, I cannot endorse the somewhat negative verdict on Brousson presented by the author. Had he consulted Baird's work, he would have noted that a key pro-Rome source document used by him is highly suspect.

6

Antoine Court

While many are familiar with the great 'Anglo-American' evangelical awakening of the eighteenth century, too little is known in the English-speaking world of the revival of French Protestantism during the same period. Occurring in significantly more hostile conditions, events in France provided a glorious proof of Christ's words regarding his church: "the gates of hell shall not prevail against it" (*Matt. 16:18*). Indeed, such opposition was never more aptly described than in the case of the sufferings of the French Reformed churches following the Revocation of the Edict of Nantes (1685).

What is more remarkable than the scale and nature of the atrocities committed against the Huguenots is the survival and then revival of the Reformed Faith. Notwithstanding the fact that diabolical persecution had produced widespread abjuration among those who would not, or could not, join the refugees, the last years of the seventeenth century testify to the amazing and heroic fortitude of many remaining pastors, elders and people—men and women, old and young. In the south of France especially, the threat of imprisonment, torture, the galleys and violent death occasioned extraordinary displays of the grace of God in the midst of sufferings quite unmatched in the history of Christianity.

Dating from 1688, the crescendo of persecution produced a 'charismatic' fanaticism among a largely pastorless people. These prophesyings—in which women and children featured prominently—became a desperate yet deceptive remedy for the oppressed. The courageous return to France of several refugee pastors helped to steady the chaotic situation to some degree. However, despair returned following the martyrdom of the 'apostolic' Claude Brousson, executed at Montpellier on 4 November 1698. While the sufferings of this servant of Christ were immortalized in the hearts and memories of Huguenot people, the years of unchecked persecution took their toll. Even the sanctified human nature of Reformed believers was at breaking point. Thus the early years of the eighteenth-century were disfigured by a resort to the sword known as the Camisard revolt (1702–4). Despite the heroic exploits of 'Roland' Laporte and Jean Cavalier, leaders of about three-thousand of Europe's first guerilla fighters against royal troops more than ten times their number, the insurrection was cruelly put down. The struggle persisted spasmodically, finally ending in 1710. However, King Louis XIV and his ministers were forced to acknowledge that Protestantism was not a spent force, despite all the measures used to exterminate it.

Son of Calvin

Even the most optimistic Huguenot could not have predicted the 'miracle' of 1715. In the very year of the king's death, a teenager from the Vivarais (modern Ardèche) was stirred at the prospect of restoring French Protestantism. He was indeed the Huguenot Nehemiah. Born at Villeneuve-de-Berg (about 20 km west of Montelimar) on 17 May, 1696, Antoine Court was destined to accomplish great things for God. His father dying when he was four years old, Antoine was blessed with a tender-hearted mother of strong Protestant convictions. At her knees he was taught the Word of God. His convictions were reinforced by the account of Rey's and Brousson's martyrdom and the exploits of the Camisards.

Like many Protestant children, Antoine was compelled to attend the local Jesuit school. Though young in years, he abhorred the Mass, the symbol of Rome's priestly power and cruelty. Since he was the only Protestant scholar at the school, the others ganged up against him. Antoine was laughed at, spat upon and stoned. As he went home, the Catholic boys shouted "Ha! Ha! eldest son of Calvin!" On one occason, four of them went to his house to force him to attend Mass. Despite their combined attempts to drag him from the stair-rails, Antoine stubbornly shook them off.

Since the Huguenot temples had been demolished at the Revocation, believers gathered by night in remote woods and rocky ravines for Reformed worship. Young Antoine was anxious to attend these secret assemblies of the 'desert church'. One evening, when his mother set out for the meeting, Antoine was determined to follow her. Reprimanded for leaving the house, he replied, "I follow you mother and I wish you to permit me to go where you go. I know that you go to pray to God, and will you refuse me the favour of going to do so with you?" Moved to tears, his mother warned him of the dangers involved. Too young and weak to walk the whole journey, a man in the group hoisted Antoine on to his shoulders and carried him the rest of the way.

Rather than violate his conscience, Antoine refused to 'pay' his way to higher education at a nearby Jesuit college by attending the Mass. While others encouraged him to pursue a trade, he had a thirst for divine truth. Besides the Bible, Antoine's convictions and experience were deepened by reading books by the great Huguenot pastor Charles Drelincourt (1595–1669) and the famous Puritan Richard Baxter (1615–91). The Baxter work was *La voix de Dieu*, a translation of the popular *Call to the Unconverted* (1658). At the age of seventeen, Antoine Court's abilities and zeal were becoming more apparent. He began to read the Bible at the assemblies. On one occasion he began to preach, much to the acceptance of the hearers. Encouraged to exercise his gift more widely, Court was determined to minister to the afflicted Protestants. A naturally anxious mother became willing to release her son for God's service when Court quoted Christ's words, "Whoever loves father and mother more than me, is not worthy of me" (*Matt. 10:37*).

Commencing an itinerant ministry, Court preached throughout Languedoc and Dauphiné. Despite dangers from spies, priests and dragoons, Court and other preachers ministered to the assemblies. Making his way to Marseille, he managed to penetrate the royal galleys. Without being detected, Court secretly ministered to the hundreds of Huguenot galley slaves. His activities becoming known, he was hotly pursued by spies. He escaped to the mountains of the Cévennes and the Vivarais, gathering large 'desert' congregations wherever he went. This relentless activity took its toll on the young man's health. During enforced rest, Court reflected on measures to revive the Reformed churches of France. Although he was only nineteen years old, having received little formal education and already being hunted by the priests and soldiers, Court was resolute. Looking back on this time, he wrote: "Young as I was, I yet foresaw all the terrible consequences of such a choice; but the firm persuasion that God would watch over me and grant me his protection so long as I did not render myself unworthy of it, confirmed my resolution. It seemed to me that nothing could be too dear to sacrifice for a church for which the Son of God had yielded up his life on the accursed tree, and nothing more glorious for me than to lose mine for his sake."

As Court evaluated the recent past, he was convinced that the interests of French Protestantism had not been well served by either the 'military' or 'fanatical' options. Following in the footsteps of Claude Brousson, he believed that obedience to the Word of God and trust in divine providence was the only way to restore the Reformed churches. Thus with a clear vision, a unique organising genius and incomparable zeal, Court dedicated himself to the work of God. Gathering a group of preachers around him, Court presided over the first synod of the Reformed churches since the national synod of Loudun (1659)—the last to be held before the Revocation. Thus Court succeeded the illustrious Jean Daillé (1594–1670). This new synod was held on 21 August 1715 at Montèze near Monoblet (in the vicinity of Nîmes), just ten days before Louis XIV expired at Versailles! After prayer, Court proposed the reorganizing of the scattered sheep of the Lord. This involved the restoration of the presbyterial discipline of the Reformed churches. Elders were appointed from among those present and regulations drawn up. They reaffirmed the *Confession of Faith* (1559) and authorized the use of Drelincourt's *Catechism* (1642). The preachers were then charged to go forth and stir up the people, especially those who had abjured. Measures were also proposed to discourage the prophesyings and silence the prophetesses. A sacred poignancy belongs to this event, not least because most of those present including Etienne Arnaud were to gain a martyr's crown.

Desert pastor

The youthful Court seems to have been the most active of the preachers. During all weathers and battling against fatigue and sometimes ill-health, his intrepid labours were astonishing. Between one desert meeting and the next, often attended by thousands of worshippers, Court moved swiftly from place to place. Sometimes he came close to capture. When preparing a sermon in a wood near Nîmes, the sound of soldiers sent him hurriedly up a tree until the danger was passed. On another occasion, hiding beneath a dungheap was the only way to evade the dragoons. Once he was staying with a friend when the house was surrounded by troops. While his friend went to bed pretending to be ill, Court hid in the narrow space between the bedstead and the wall. On bursting into the house, the soldiers examined every likely hiding place except the gap behind the bed! Clearly, as Court himself believed, God's amazing providence was at work.

After serving as a preacher for three years, Court was ordained as a pastor. His old friend, the preacher Pierre Corteiz had received ordination in Zurich. Corteiz then ordained Court at a ceremony held in the Vaunage on the night of 21 November 1718. He was now authorized with the authority of the synod to exercise all the functions of the ministry. Redoubling his energies in the Lord's work, Court was anxious to nourish the faith of the people with sound literature. "Our need of books is very great," he wrote to a friend abroad. After the Revocation, the authorities had seized and burned Protestant Bibles, Psalters, catechisms and other books. Piles were consigned to the flames in every town. Louis XV perpetuated the same policy and immense piles were again destroyed. Refugees in the Netherlands, Switzerland and England responded generously to meet the need. Besides Bibles, Psalters and catechisms, devotional works by Drelincourt, the great Jean Claude (1619–87) and others were sent into France.

Court also saw the importance of theological education for

the preachers. When applicants were approved—"good, virtuous men, full of zeal for the cause of truth", as he wrote to Pierre Durand (martyred in 1732)—they had to be well trained. Since the Genevese feared the wrath of France, Court could not depend on the academy there. He therefore resorted to a more basic approach. "I have often pitched my professor's chair in a torrent underneath a rock," he wrote. "The sky was our roof, and the leafy branches thrown out from the crevices in the rock overhead, were our canopy." Based on the French Reformed Confession (drawn up chiefly by Calvin), a rigorous theological programme included an exacting homiletic training. "When the more advanced students were required to preach, they mounted a particular place, where a pole had been set across some rocks in the ravine, and which for the time served for a pulpit. And when they had delivered themselves, the others were requested by turns to express themseves freely upon the subject of the sermon which they had heard."

Court's Calvinism

Court was obviously careful to provide sound theological guidance for his students.Having noted that he had read Richard Baxter's *Call to the Unconverted* in his youth, one wonders where he stood on the question of Calvinism. As we have seen, the work appeared in several French editions as *La voix de Dieu*. Court very possibly read the fifth edition, published rather appropriately at Saumur in 1680. In language which Calvin, Amyraut and, judging by his catechism, Drelincourt would have approved of, Court would have learned from Baxter that, notwithstanding the biblical doctrine of election, the death of Christ was—according to equally-plain scripture—not 'only for the elect. For it was…the sin of all the world that lay upon our redeemer; and his sacrifice and satisfaction is sufficient for all, and the fruits of it are offered to one as well as to another…' In the absence of any hard evidence to the contrary, and consistent with his future work in Lausanne, such was very probably the character of Court's Calvinism.

While funds offered by the faithful were scarce, young men were never wanting to supply the places of the martyred preachers. Court himself shared the austere conditions of his brethren. His labours were prodigious. During a two-month period, he visited thirty-one churches in Lower Languedoc and the Cévennes. Travelling over three hundred miles (480 km), he held 'desert' assemblies, preaching and administering the sacraments. By the year 1729, there were over 200,000 confessing Protestants in Languedoc alone. Though secretly governed, there were forty churches in Languedoc, eighteen in the Cévennes, twelve in Lozère and forty-two in the Vivarais. In all, one hundred and twenty churches had been re-established, each with an eldership and supported by a provincial synod. Despite the cruel oppression of new royal edicts against the Huguenots, the movement spread to other parts of France. Dauphiné in the south-east, Béarn and Guienne in the south-west, Saintonge and Poitou in the west, and Normandy and Picardy in the far north felt the heaven-blest influence of Antoine Court and his brethren.

Seminary professor

For some time, Court cherished the possibility of setting up a ministerial academy in a less vulnerable situation. The providence of God was to make this a reality. After marrying a young Huguenot woman in 1722, Court's home at Uzès became the base for his activities. To avoid jeopardizing his ministry, he visited his wife and three children secretly. Suspicions were aroused in the neighbourhood since Mme Court was known as a woman of godly reputation. When the new commandant of Uzès made searching enquiries about the woman's husband, Court acted to remove them from danger. Making arrangements for them to escape to Geneva, Court's family reached the city in April 1729. Continuing to preach in Languedoc, Court became seriously ill. Utterly exhausted and anxious for his family, he made a hazardous journey to join them in Geneva. This development enabled Court to realise his objective. Despite the expostulations of his brethren—who even began to doubt his courage (!), Court was determined to serve the cause of God in ways they failed to envisage. Eventually settling with his family in Lausanne, he opened a seminary there. Until his death thirty years later, Court prepared the zealous and single-minded youths of Languedoc and the Vivarais for ministry and often martyrdom in the service of Christ and his suffering saints. The number of itinerant pastors steadily grew. By 1756 there were forty-eight pastors at work with twenty-two probationary preachers and students.

The restored churches were spared neither periodic persecution nor internal dissensions. Asked to mediate in a case of pastoral misconduct, Court made a precarious journey to Languedoc in 1744. Still with a price on his head, his return was hailed with immense rejoicing. Preaching to vast crowds wherever he went, Court remained in France for about a month. Despite excessive heat and wearisome travel, and never without danger, he saw widespread evidence of the blessing of God. Arriving at a prearranged location near Montpellier well after midnight, Court was greeted by a large and enthusiastic assembly. "I dismounted," he wrote, "put on my gown, ascended the pulpit [a portable device used on such occasions], and preached with as much power as though I had come straight from my study." Near Sauzet (20 km south-east of Anduze), nearly twenty-thousand people assembled. At this national synod, the pastoral schism was resolved. When the reconciled parties embraced one another, the whole assembly broke forth into a psalm. Court later preached to nearly seven-thousand souls in a grove near Alès. "The scene under the tents was beautiful," he recorded, "there was great rejoicing when I appeared in the pulpit." Returning to Lausanne in October 1744, Court wrote: 'I have left the Protestants full of zeal, and in a state incomparably better than at any time since the Revocation."

Paul Rabaut

Antoine Court's wife died in 1755. Keenly feeling his loss, this intrepid servant of Christ laboured on. He died on the 15 June 1760. Brilliantly followed in the seminary by his son Court Gebelin, Court's acknowledged successor among the churches was the equally remarkable Paul Rabaut (1718–94). Under his wise and zealous leadership, the restored Reformed churches of France became established. Notwithstanding occasional continuing persecution, they finally obtained religious liberty in the Edict of Toleration (1787), granted by Louis XVI on the eve of the French Revolution (1789). Truly, the 'gates of hell' did not prevail against the true church. On the contrary, the royal despotism that had oppressed it perished in the divine judgement of the Reign of Terror. Indeed, Court and his comrades in the faith proved repeatedly, that none can withstand Him who declared, "All power is given unto me in heaven and on earth" (*Matt. 28:18*).

Having focused particularly on the pioneering labours of John Calvin, the pastoral faithfulness of Amyraut and Daillé, the noble sufferings of Brousson and Rey, and the revival exploits of Antoine Court, we may see them as representatives of a 'noble army' of French Reformed servants of our Lord Jesus Christ. Smiles reminds us that between the year 1686, when Fulchran Rey was hanged at Beaucaire, and the year 1698, when Claude Brousson was hanged at Montpellier, no fewer than seventeen pastors were publicly executed at various locations. Even if one were to ignore the horrors of the St Bartholomew massacre of 1572, and other persecutions before and after, these facts alone are sufficient to indict the Roman Catholic Church for being a blatant antichristian organisation. Even then, such suffering continued for more than half a century, even beyond the lifetime of Antoine Court!

The efforts of the French historian M. De Felice to absolve the people of France in general for the barbarities that occurred over so long a period, as if only the monarchy, the royal advisers and the priests were guilty, are not persuasive. The inescapable verdict is that those educated by the Jesuits and their collaborators were complicit in Catholic-inspired crimes, and that, as Smiles comments on the significance of the French Revolution, 'in 1793, the people educated by these [perfidious teachers] treated King, Jesuits, priests and aristocracy, in precisely the same manner that they had treated the Huguenots'. On a final positive note, when all is said and done, Huguenot history provides the most powerful vindication of authentic Christianity the world has ever known.

Further reading:

Baird, H. M., *The Huguenots and the Revocation of the Edict of Nantes* (London: Hodder & Stoughton, 1895).

Clifford, A. C., *Atonement and Justification: English Evangelical Theology 1640–1790—An Evaluation* (Oxford: OUP, 1990, 2002).

——*Calvinus: Authentic Calvinism, A Clarification* (Norwich: Charenton Reformed Publishing, 1996; 2nd ed. 2007).

——*Amyraut Affirmed* (Norwich: Charenton Reformed Publishing, 2004).

Grant, A. J., *The Huguenots* (London: Thornton Butterworth Ltd., 1934).

Gray, J. G., *The French Huguenots: Anatomy of Courage*
(Grand Rapids: Baker Book House, 1981).

Gwynn, R. D., *Huguenot Heritage* (London: Routledge, 1985).

Hugues, E., *Antoine Court Histoire de la Restauration du Protestantisme en France au XVIIIe siècle* (Paris, 1872).

——(ed), *Mémoires d'Antoine Court* (Toulouse: 1885).

Orna-Ornstein, F., *France...Forgotten Mission Field* (Welwyn: European Missionary Fellowship, 1971).

Prestwich, M. (ed), *International Calvinism, 1541–1715* (Oxford: OUP, 1985).

Smiles, S., *The Huguenots in France after the Revocation of the Edict of Nantes* (London: Dalby, isbister & Co., 1875).

Tylor, C., *The Camisards: a sequel to 'The Huguenots of the Seventeenth Century'* (London: Simpkin, Marshall, Hamilton etc., 1893).

Epilogue

Having reflected on the life and testimony of John Calvin and some of his 'sons', we conclude by considering a very fundamental question. What would they expect of us in the 21st century? Of course, our world is dominated by secular, ecumenical and multi-faith values, far removed from the outlook of those we have considered. If we pursue these modern values, then we must consign our heroes to history, admiring at best their tenacity and courage without endorsing their ideas. However, to return to the question, our heroes would urge us to perpetuate the truth they transmitted to us at such great cost. Christians who believe as they did, who insist that Christian truth is eternal, will desire to do nothing else. This is certainly my conviction. In short, believing that John Calvin remains the greatest advocate of authentic Christianity, we both recognise and declare the timeless relevance of his contribution and insights. Indeed, it is time to repeat the biblical message he proclaimed in his day, a message which challenges the very dubious modern values identified earlier. We note first some truly pertinent statements of Calvin on these issues:

1. AUTHENTIC CHRISTIANITY

THE GOSPEL ACCORDING TO CALVIN

The Complete Gospel

We have the Gospel in its entirety, when we know that He who had long been promised as Redeemer came down from heaven, put on our flesh, lived in the world, experienced death and then rose again; and secondly when we see the purpose and fruits of all these things in the fact that He was God with us, that He gave us in Himself a sure pledge of our adoption, that by the grace of His Spirit He has cleansed us from the stains of our carnal iniquities and consecrated us to be temples to God, that He has raised us from the depths to heaven, that by His sacrificial death He has made atonement for the sins of the world, that He has reconciled us to the Father, and that He has been the source of righteousness and life for us. Whoever holds to these things has rightly grasped the Gospel (*Comment on 2 Peter 1:16*).

Justification by Faith

God ... receives the full and complete praise which is His due only as He alone obtains the name and honour of being just, while the whole human race is condemned of unrighteousness. The other part refers to the communication of righteousness, for God does not by any means shut His riches within Himself, but pours them forth upon mankind. The righteousness of God, therefore, shines in us in so far as He justifies us by faith in Christ, for Christ was given in vain for our righteousness, if there were no enjoyment of Him by faith. It follows from this that in themselves all men are unrighteous and lost, until a remedy from heaven was offered to them (*Comment on Rom. 3:26*).

Again, if it is a definition of the righteousness of faith to say, 'Blessed are they whose iniquities are forgiven' (*Ps. 32:1*), there is no dispute about different kinds of works, but the merit of works is abolished, and the remission of sins alone is established as the cause of righteousness (*Comment on Rom. 3:21*).

Christ by His obedience satisfied the judgement of the Father.... Our guilt is taken away by the expiatory sacrifice which He offered (*Comment on Rom. 3:24*).

When, however, we come to Christ, we first find in Him the exact righteousness of the law, and this also becomes ours by imputation (*Comment on Rom. 3:31*).

....righteousness for Paul is nothing other than the remission of sins,...(*Comment on Rom. 4:6*).

....our righteousness has been procured by the obedience of Christ which He displayed in His death,... (*Comment on Rom. 4:25*)

… Christ has attained righteousness for sinners by His death, … (*Comment on Rom. 5:5*)

When he….states that we are made righteous by the obedience of Christ, we deduce from this that Christ, in satisfying the Father, has procured righteousness for us (*Comment on Rom. 5:19*).

Likewise, by the word grace we understand both parts of redemption, i.e. the forgiveness of sins, by which God imputes righteousness to us, and sanctification of the Spirit, by whom He forms us anew to good works (*Comment on Rom. 6:14*).

Christ, the Pope, Muhammad & Others

Muhammad and the Pope have this religious principle in common, that Scripture does not contain the perfection of doctrine, but that something higher has been revealed by the Spirit. The Anabaptists and Libertines have in our own day drawn their madness from the same ditch (*Comment on John 14:25*).

This error [of additional revelation beyond Christ] is followed by another, no less intolerable; that having said goodbye to Christ's law, as if His reign were ended, and He now nothing at all, they substitute the Spirit in His place. From this source have flowed the sacrileges of the Papacy and Muhammadanism. For although those antichrists are dissimilar in many respects they have a common starting point: that in the Gospel we are initiated into the true faith, but that the perfection of doctrine must be sought elsewhere, to perfect us completely. If Scripture is brought against the Pope, he denies that we should keep to it, since the Spirit has also now come and has lifted us above it by many additions. Muhammad proclaims that without his *Qur'an* men always remain children. Thus, by a false claim to the Spirit, the world has been bewitched to leave the simple purity of Christ. For as soon as the Spirit is severed from Christ's Word the door is open to all sorts of craziness and impostures. Many fanatics have tried a similar method of deception in our own age. The written teaching seems to them to be of the letter. Therefore they were pleased to make up a new theology consisting of revelations (*Comment on John 16:14*).

The Papists boast with professorial superciliousness that all their inventions are the oracles of the Spirit. Muhammad, too, asserts that he has drawn his dreams only from heaven. In olden times the Egyptians lied that the mad absurdities with which they bewitched themselves and others had been divinely revealed. But I reply that we have the Word of the Lord [the Holy Bible], which should be consulted first (*Comment on 1 John 4:6*).

Christ and Mary

'Jesus said to [His mother], "Woman, what does your concern have to do with me? My hour has not yet come." His mother said to the servants, "Whatever He says to you, do it." '(*John 2:4–5*)

[Mary] sinned by going beyond her proper bounds. ... Christ spoke like this not so much for her sake as for others. ... It is certain that this saying of Christ openly warns men not to transfer to Mary what belongs to God, by superstitiously exalting the honour of the maternal name in Mary. Christ therefore addresses His mother like this so as to transmit a perpetual and general lesson to all ages, lest an extravagant honour paid to His mother should obscure His divine glory.

How necessary this warning became, in consequence of the gross and abominable superstitions which followed later, is known well enough. For Mary has been made Queen of Heaven, the Hope, the Life and Salvation of the world; and in fact, their insane raving went so far that they just stripped Christ and adorned her with the spoils. And when we condemn those accursed blasphemies against the Son of God, the Papists call us malicious and envious. Nay, they spread the wicked slander that we are deadly foes to the honour of the holy virgin. As if she had not all the honour that belongs to her without being made a goddess! As if it were honouring her to adorn her with sacrilegious titles and put her in Christ's place! It is they who do Mary a cruel injury when they snatch from God what belongs to Him that they may deform her with false praises.

[Mary's] statement has a wider application [to that present situation]. For she first disclaims and lays aside the power she might seem to have usurped, and then she ascribes all power to Christ alone when she tells [the servants] to follow His command. Hence, we are taught here in general that if we desire anything from Christ we shall not obtain our prayers unless we depend entirely on Him and, in short, do whatever He commands. But He does not send us away to His mother but invites us to Himself (*Comment on John 2:4–5*).

A Prayer for Loyalty to Christ

Grant, Almighty God, that since Your Son has been made known to us, through Whom is brought to us the perfection of all blessings, and of true and real glory,—O grant, that we might continue settled in Him, and never turn here and there, nor fluctuate in any way, but be so satisfied with His Kingship and Priesthood, as to deliver up ourselves wholly to His care and protection, and never doubt but that we are so sanctified by His grace as to be now acceptable to You, and that relying on Him as our Mediator, we might offer ourselves as a sacrifice to You with full confidence of heart, and thus strive to glorify You through the whole course of our life, that we might at length be made partakers of that celestial glory which has been obtained for us by the blood of Your only-begotten Son.—Amen.

2. THE AUTHENTIC CHURCH

Having embraced the biblical apostolic doctrine of faith and order maintained by Calvin and his 'sons', we resolutely resist, in the following manner, the imperious claims of the religious organisation that persecuted them:

Conversion to the Roman Catholic Church is surely a retrograde and tragic step. While the apostate condition of many Protestant Churches gives sufficient cause for disillusionment, the Roman option cannot provide a safe or satisfying spiritual home. As affirmed in the doctrinal declaration *Dominus Iesus* (2000), Rome's claims to be the only 'correct' church could not be more invalid. The proof is as follows:

I The doctrines of the Roman Church are utterly inconsistent with the plain teaching of the New Testament. The finality of Christ's unique sacrifice and His priestly intercession (see *Hebrews 9:28; 10:11–12*) rule out the sacrifice of the mass and a human priesthood. The theory of transubstantiation is an absurd philosophical fiction and utterly detrimental to the simple symbolism of the Lord's Supper—a memorial of our Saviour's once-for-all sacrifice. Thus His blood shedding is remembered not repeated, on a table not an altar (hence ministers are pastors not priests); His real presence is spiritual, not physical, in the hearts of His people and not in the bread and wine.

II Justification by faith in Christ's merit alone (see *Romans 5:1–9*) and direct access to Him as sole Mediator (see *Matthew 11:28; 1 Timothy 2:5*) rule out the false and pretentious teaching that Mary is Mediatrix, Auxiliatrix, Advocatrix, Queen of Heaven, etc. The idea that the merits of the faithful are a necessary contribution to their salvation undermines the all-sufficiency of Christ's merit. Rome's traditional mistake in making sanctification a part of justification arises from her reliance on the Latin *justificare* instead of the Greek *dikaioo*. While the former verb means 'to make righteous', the latter means 'to declare righteous' by the remission of sins through faith in the blood of Christ (see *Romans 4:5–8; 5:1, 9*). While good works are a necessary and certain fruit of saving faith (see *Galatians 5:6; Ephesians 2:8–10*), their imperfection rules them out from justifying us. Our persons and our performances alike always require pardon. That said, Christian sainthood is the present status of true though imperfect believers (see *Ephesians 1:1–2*) not that of dead believers canonised by the Church of Rome.

III Thus purgatory and prayers for the dead (including requiem masses) have no apostolic warrant. Those who die 'in Christ' have no need of our prayers. Those who die otherwise cannot be helped by them. Besides corrupting Baptism and the Holy Communion, Rome arrogantly added five more supposed sacraments to those commanded by Christ. Her realignment of the Ten Commandments—combining the first two and dividing the tenth—obscure in summary form God's prohibition of the idolatry of such popular graven images as crucifixes and statues of Mary, etc. Other distortions of divine truth are no less serious. The Pope's title 'Holy Father' is a blasphemous insult to God the Father (see *John 17:11*). His claim to be the 'vicar of Christ' is a further insult to the Holy Spirit, Christ's true representative on earth (see *John 14:16–17*). Indeed, for all its profession of the Holy

Trinity, Rome's doctrine of salvation tramples on Trinitarian truth. The political claims of a highly fallible Papacy conflict with Christ's words that His kingdom 'is not of this world' (*John 18:36*). Rome's growing ambition to dominate Europe as in the days of the Holy Roman Empire is a re-emerging tyranny to be resisted by individual Christians and national governments alike. Her arrogance is at odds with Christ's liberating truth (see *John 8:32, 36; Galatians 5:1*).

IV In addition to theological objections, the track record of Roman Catholicism does not commend itself. For violent and bloody persecution, no organization can compete with Rome. Since the true Church of Christ is 'persecuted' rather than 'persecutor', this one consideration alone makes Rome's claim to 'correctness' null and void (see *John 15:20–1; 2 Timothy 3:12*). Besides the burnings of the sixteenth-century British reformers, the dreadful cruelties inflicted on the ancient Waldensians, the French Huguenots, the Dutch Protestants and others (including Jews, Muslims and Eastern Orthodox) have never been truly repented of—since the doctrine directing these atrocities remains in tact. Indeed, under another name—'The Congregation for the Doctrine of the Faith', the Inquisition still exists. Current persecution of Protestants in Central and South America shows no change in Rome's methods where she has a free hand. The intrigue and corrupting influence of the Jesuits knows no parallel. Vatican complicity in the rise of Hitler and the Nazi holocaust is well attested. The evils of the confessional and the 'unholy wedlock' of supposedly celibate priests refute Rome's sanctimonious image. While marital failure among protestant pastors is to be lamented, is it any wonder that paedophilia and HIV are rife among sexually-frustrated and homosexual Roman priests?

V Considering the post-reformation dogmas of Mary's immaculate conception (1854), papal infallibility (1870) and the Assumption of Mary (1950), the Church of Rome is even more apostate than she was in Luther's day. Thus any form of ecumenism on Rome's terms is nothing but satanic delusion (see *2 Thessalonians 2:1–12*). Especially in the wake of *Dominus Iesus*, when naïve and gullible evangelicals, charismatics and others try to persuade us that 'Rome is changing', ask them which of her anti-biblical dogmas has

Rome renounced? May all God's people understand the 'signs of the times' and cease not 'contending earnestly for the faith once delivered to the saints' (*Jude 3*). Amen!

3. AUTHENTIC CALVINISM

Consistent with what I have argued in several publications, I make no apology for having asserted in the present work that Amyraut and his associates are the true heirs of Calvin's Bible-based, Christ-exalting evangelistic theology. Those who tend to dismiss the ubiquitous universal atonement language of the reformer usually do the same with the universal language of the biblical texts. All too often, an over-exaggerated concern to protect God's sovereignty in salvation produces a dishonest exegesis of the kind Calvin would never recognise. Indeed, all textual tampering would incur his justifiable wrath. Unable to embrace antinomy in their theology, our scholastic rationalists end up deleting the obvious presence of 'tension' between the universal and particular features of biblical soteriology. Lack of balance in Beza's distortion of Calvin's legacy led predictably to the equally-unbalanced Arminian reaction. Sadly, this theological divide has had a detrimental effect on evangelistic endeavour and Christian unity, in several respects. It is my conviction that numerous problems in theory and practice are avoided if only we perpetuate Calvin's numerous utterances on this subject. It is liberating to find that all the objections to Calvinism as being inherently opposed to evangelism and missionary endeavour simply evaporate when we allow John Calvin to speak for himself! I close with a few examples of 'authentic Calvinism' (referring the reader to my *Calvinus* for bibliographical details):

Extracts from John Calvin on the extent of the

atonement and predestination

It is incontestable that Christ came for the expiation of the sins of the whole world. But the solution lies close at hand, that whosoever believes in Him should not perish but should have eternal life (*Jn.*

3:15)... Hence, we conclude that, though reconciliation is offered to all through Him, yet the benefit is peculiar to the elect, that they may be gathered into the society of life. However, while I say it is offered to all, I do not mean that this embassy, by which on Paul's testimony (*2 Cor. 5:18*) God reconciles the world to Himself, reaches to all, but that it is not sealed indiscriminately on the hearts of all to whom it comes so as to be effectual (*Concerning the Eternal Predestination of God*).

Now we must see how God wishes all to be converted...But we must remark that God puts on a twofold character: for he here wishes to be taken at his word. As I have already said, the Prophet does not here dispute with subtlety about his incomprehensible plans, but wishes to keep our attention close to God's word. Now what are the contents of this word? The law, the prophets, and the gospel. Now all are called to repentance, and the hope of salvation is promised them when they repent: this is true, since God rejects no returning sinner: he pardons all without exception; meanwhile, this will of God which he sets forth in his word does not prevent him from decreeing before the world was created what he would do with every individual (*Comment on Ezekiel 18:23*).

I contend that, as the prophet [Ezekiel] is exhorting to penitence, it is no wonder that he pronounces God willing that all be saved. But the mutual relation between threats and promises shows such forms of speech to be conditional... So again...the promises which invite all men to salvation...do not simply and positively declare what God has decreed in His secret counsel but what he is prepared to do for all who are brought to faith and repentance...Now this is not contradictory of His secret counsel, by which he determined to convert none but His elect. He cannot rightly on this account be thought variable, because as lawgiver He illuminates all with the external doctrine of life. But in the other sense, he brings to life whom He will, as Father regenerating by the Spirit only His sons (*Concerning the Eternal Predestination of God*).

First, we must understand that as long as Christ remains outside of us, and we are separated from him, all that he has suffered and done for the salvation of the human race remains useless and of no value for us (*Institutes, III. i. 1*).

For God, who is perfect righteousness, cannot love the iniquity which he sees in all. All of us, therefore, have that within which deserves the hatred of God…Our acquittal is in this—that the guilt which made us liable to punishment was transferred to the head of the Son of God [Isa. 53:12]…For, were not Christ a victim, we could have no sure conviction of his being…our substitute-ransom and propitiation (*Institutes II. xvi. 3, 5, 6*).

True it is that the effect of [Christ's] death comes not to the whole world. Nevertheless, forasmuch as it is not in us to discern between the righteous and the sinners that go to destruction, but that Jesus Christ has suffered his death and passion as well for them as for us, therefore it behoves us to labour to bring every man to salvation, that the grace of our Lord Jesus Christ may be available to them (*Sermons on Job*).

Yet I approve of the common reading, that He alone bore the punishment of many, because the guilt of the whole world was laid upon Him. It is evident from other passages…that 'many' sometimes denotes 'all' …That, then, is how our Lord Jesus bore the sins and iniquities of many. But in fact, this word 'many' is often as good as equivalent to 'all'. And indeed, our Lord Jesus was offered to all the world. For it is not speaking of three or four when it says: 'God so loved the world, that He spared not His only Son.' But yet we must notice what the Evangelist adds in this passage: 'That whosoever believes in Him shall not perish but obtain eternal life.' Our Lord Jesus suffered for all and there is neither great nor small who is not inexcusable today, for we can obtain salvation in Him. Unbelievers who turn away from Him and who deprive themselves of Him by their malice are today doubly culpable. For how will they excuse their ingratitude in not receiving the blessing in which they could share by faith? And let us realize that if we come flocking to our Lord Jesus Christ, we shall not hinder one another and prevent Him being sufficient for each of us…Let us not fear to come to Him in great numbers, and each one of us bring his neighbours, seeing that He is sufficient to save us all (*Sermons on Isaiah 53*).

Not only were the death and passion of our Lord Jesus Christ sufficient for the salvation of the world, but that God will make them efficacious and that we shall see the fruit of them and even feel and experience it (*Sermons on Isaiah 53*).

Our Lord made effective for [the pardoned thief on the cross] His death and passion which He suffered and endured for all mankind...(*Sermons on Christ's Passion*).

Moreover, we offer up our prayers unto Thee, O most Gracious God and most merciful Father, for all men in general, that as Thou art pleased to be acknowledged the Saviour of the whole human race by the redemption accomplished by Jesus Christ Thy Son, so those who are still strangers to the knowledge of him, and immersed in darkness, and held captive by ignorance and error, may, by Thy Holy Spirit shining upon them, and by Thy gospel sounding in their ears, be brought back to the right way of salvation, which consists in knowing Thee the true God and Jesus Christ whom Thou hast sent...(*Forms of Prayer for the Church*).

And surely there is nothing that ought to be more effective in spurring on pastors to devote themselves more eagerly to their duty than if they reflect that it is to themselves that the price of the blood of Christ has been entrusted. For it follows from this, that unless they are faithful in putting out their labour on the Church, not only are they made accountable for lost souls, but they are guilty of sacrilege, because they have profaned the sacred blood of the Son of God, and have made useless the redemption acquired by Him, as far as they are concerned. But it is a hideous and monstrous crime if, by our idleness, not only the death of Christ becomes worthless, but also the fruit of it is destroyed and perishes... (*Comment on Acts 20:28*).

Paul makes grace common to all men, not because it in fact extends to all, but because it is offered to all. Although Christ suffered for the sins of the world, and is offered by the goodness of God without distinction to all men, yet not all receive him (*Comment on Romans 5:18*).

It is not enough to regard Christ as having died for the salvation of the world; each man must claim the effect and possession of this grace for himself personally (*Comment on Galatians 2:20*).

God commends to us the salvation of all men without exception, even as Christ suffered for the sins of the whole world (*Comment on Galatians 5:12*).

To bear the sins means to free those who have sinned from their guilt by his satisfaction. He says many meaning all, as in Rom. 5:15. It is of course certain that not all enjoy the fruits of Christ's death, but this happens because their unbelief hinders them (*Comment on Hebrews 9:27*).

This is His wondrous love towards the human race, that He desires all men to be saved, and is prepared to bring even the perishing to safety...It could be asked here, if God does not want any to perish, why do so many in fact perish? My reply is that no mention is made here of the secret decree of God by which the wicked are doomed to their own ruin, but only of His loving-kindness as it is made known to us in the Gospel. There God stretches out His hand to all alike, but He only grasps those (in such a way as to lead to Himself) whom He has chosen before the foundation of the world (*Comment on 2 Peter 3:9*).

[Him God set forth to be a propitiation through faith in his blood for our sins, and not for ours only, but also for the sins of the whole world...But though he died for all, all do not receive the benefit of his death, but those only to whom the merit of his passion is communicated... (*Articles III, IV of the Sixth Session of the Council of Trent*)]

The third and fourth heads I do not touch... (*Antidote to the Council of Trent*).

...Christ, who is the salvation of the world,... (*Catechism of the Church of Geneva*)

I John Calvin, servant of the Word of God in the church of Geneva, weakened by many illnesses...thank God that he has not only shown mercy to me, his poor creature...and suffered me in all sins and weaknesses, but what is more than that, he has made me a partaker of his grace to serve him through my work...I confess to live and die in this faith which he has given me, inasmuch as I have no other hope or refuge than his predestination upon which my entire salvation is grounded. I embrace the grace which he has offered me in our Lord Jesus Christ, and accept the merits of his suffering and dying that through him all my sins are buried; and I humbly beg him to wash me and cleanse me with the blood of our great Redeemer, as it was shed for all poor sinners so that I, when I appear before his face, may bear his likeness (*Calvin's Last Will: April 25, 1564*).

SOLI DEO GLORIA

They Had Their Enemies: High Anglican Antipathy Unveiled
In April, 1668. Dr. Creighton, Dean of Wells [1593–1672], the most famous, loquacious, ready-tongu'd Preacher of the Court, who was used to preach Calvin to Hell, and the Calvinists to the Gallows; and by his scornful reviling and jests, to set the Court on a Laughter, was suddenly, in the pulpit, (without any sickness) surprized with Astonishment, … and when he had repeated a Sentence over and over, and was so confounded, that he could go no further at all, he was fain, to all Men's wonder, to come down. And his case was more wonderful than almost any other Man's, being not only a fluent, extemporate Speaker, but one that was never known to want words, especially to express his Satyrical or bloody Thoughts.

[Samuel Parker, 1640-88, bp. of Oxford, 1668, an 'ex-sectarian' conformist, 'who turned with the times'], in his 'virulent book' *Ecclesiastical Policy* (1670) … with the most voluminous torrent of natural and malicious Rhetoric [spoke] over the same things which might have been Comprised in a few Sentences; viz. The *Nonconformists, Calvinists, Presbyterians, Hugonots*, are the most villainous unsufferable sort of sanctified Fools, Knaves; and unquiet Rebels that ever were in the World: With their naughty Godliness, and Hypocrisie and Villanies, making it necessary to fall upon their Teachers, and not to spare them; for the Conquering of the rest. But yet he putteth more exceptions here of the Soberer, honest, peaceable sort (whom he loveth but pittyeth for the unhappiness of their education) and in particular speaketh kindly of me, than he had done before.

Richard Baxter, *Reliquiae Baxterianae or, Mr Richard Baxter's Narrative of the Most memorable Passages of his Life and Times*, ed. N. H. Keeble, et al (Oxford University Press, 2020), ii. 363, 375–6.

The Profound Paradox of God and his grace

[or the Gospel According to **Calvin**] and affirmed by **Amyraut**

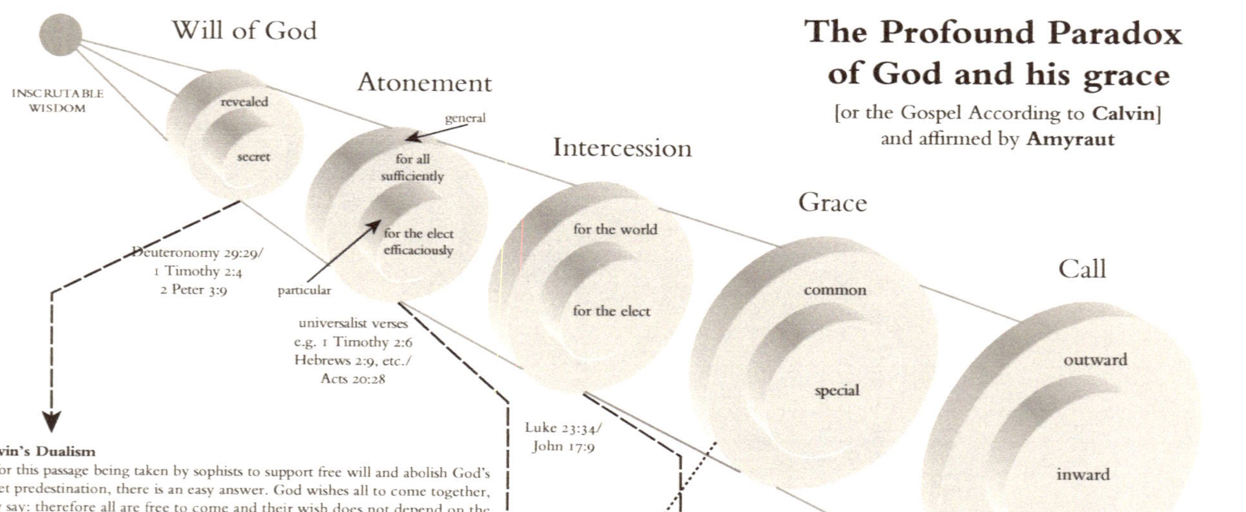

Calvin's Dualism

As for this passage being taken by sophists to support free will and abolish God's secret predestination, there is an easy answer. God wishes all to come together, they say: therefore all are free to come and their wish does not depend on the election of God. I answer, that the will of God as mentioned here must be judged by the result. Seeing that in His Word He calls **all** alike to salvation, and this is the object of preaching, that **all** should take refuge in His faith and protection, it is right to say that He wishes **all** to gather to Him. Now the nature of the Word shows us that here there is no description of the secret counsel of God (*arcanum Dei consilium*)—just His wishes. Certainly those whom He wishes effectively to gather, He draws **inwardly** by His Spirit, and calls them not merely by man's **outward** voice. If anyone objects that it is absurd to split God's will (*duplicem in Deo voluntatem fingi*), I answer that this is exactly our belief, that His will is one and undivided: but because our minds cannot plumb the profound depths of His **secret** election (*ad profundam arcanae electionis abyssum*) to suit our infirmity, the will of God is set before us as **double** (*bifariam*) *Commentary on Matthew* 23:37

Paul makes grace **common** to all men, not because it in fact extends to all, but because it is offered to **all.** Although Christ suffered for the sins of the world, and is offered by the goodness of God without distinction to all men, yet not all receive Him. *Commentary on Romans* 5:18

He openly declares that **He does not pray for the world,** for He is solicitous only for His own flock which He received from the Father's hand. But this might seem absurd; for no better rule of prayer can be found that to follow Christ as our Guide and Teacher. But we are commanded to pray for all, and **Christ Himself afterwards prayed for all indiscriminately,** 'Father, forgive them; for they know not what they do.' I reply, the prayers which we utter for all are still limited to God's elect. We ought to pray that this and that and every man may be saved and so embrace the whole human race, because we cannot yet distinguish the elect from the reprobate.

Commentary on John 17:9

Calvin describes faith as 'a **special** grace of God' (*Sermons on Ephesians,* 146) Elsewhere he says that 'unless we are by **special** grace called to be sharers of the fruit of the death and passion of the Son of God, it will be useless to us' (*Sermons on the Saving Work of Christ,* trans. L. Nixon p.100)

NOTES ON THE DIAGRAM

1. A correlation is to be noted between the small disc and large disc areas of each pair of subject circles.

2. While Arminians tend to focus on the 'large disc', Owenites (and especially Gillites) do likewise on the 'small disc'.

3. As Calvin did, Amyraldians alias Baxterians maintain a 'bifocal' emphasis.

4. Unlike the more logically-consistent particularist John Gill, Owen accepted the common/special grace distinction and the 'free offer' of the Gospel.

5. Owenites (whose 'commercial' atonement theory effectively negates its universal sufficiency) are confronted by a dilemma. If they wish to maintain the 'grace dualism' and the 'free offer', they must embrace Baxter's view of the atonement. Otherwise, they cannot logically escape the hypercalvinism of Gill.

My Opinion of Owen & Owenism

Dr John Owen was eminent in many respects. However, Calvin admirer and Dort endorser Richard Baxter rightly spoke of Owen as 'the over-orthodox doctor'. In my view, Owen's *Death of Death* (1647) was a mistake: it was not necessary and should never have been written, and equally, never republished by the Banner of Truth Trust with equally 'over-orthodox' Anglican Packer's 'Introduction' (1959). I actually refuted the Owenite view in my *Atonement and Justification* (Clarendon Press, Oxford, 1990). As well as others, Dr David L. Allen (*The Extent of the Atonement*, B&H Academic, 2016, p. 204), considers that I have answered Owen. Furthermore, the occupancy of the Owenite position within an Anglican context has no integrity. Despite an ecclesiology alien to the New Testament, Anglican soteriology is sound. The formularies (the BCP, especially the Communion prayer of consecration, Articles and Homilies) plus the well-nigh unanimity of the reformers' sermons, never committed clergy to Owen's extreme particularism. So, as was the case of Dr Packer (who failed to deliver a planned response to my *Churchman* article (1986:4), Anglican Owenites are strictly 'out of order'. From Hooker, Ussher and Davenant through to Newton, Simeon, Ryle and D. Broughton Knox, Anglican soteriology rightly affirms a 'middle ground' between Arminianism and Owenism. As for Amyraut, the secret of grasping his position is his perpetual Bible-led appeal to proto-Amyraldian Calvin. As further examples are about to reveal, Richard A. Muller's denial that Amyraut's teaching has precedents in Calvin's perspicuous teaching is not credible (Klauber (ed.), *The Theology of the French Reformed Churches* (2014), p. 205). Dr Muller generously denies that Amyraut's teaching was heretical (unlike many in the WCF camp), but denigrating his 'popular parlance' distinction between antecedent and consequent divine decrees has no validity. Akin to Calvin, Amyraut exonerated himself at his heresy trial (1637) by rejecting any temporal dimension in what may simply be styled as the 'double-aspect' single will of God.

REFORMED LITURGY

A service of worship including the celebration of

THE LORD'S SUPPER

INVOCATION
'*Our help is in the name of the Lord, who made heaven and earth*'
(Ps. 124:8).

CONFESSION OF SINS
The pastor calls upon the congregation thus:
"Brothers and sisters, let us humble ourselves before the Lord, confessing
our sins. Follow me in your minds while I lead with these words":

O LORD GOD, eternal and almighty Father, we acknowledge and sincerely confess before Your Holy Majesty that we are unworthy sinners, conceived and born in guilt and sin, prone to iniquity and, without Your grace, incapable of any good work, and that to our shame we make no end of transgressing Your commandments. We thus call down destruction upon ourselves according to Your just judgement. Nevertheless, O Lord, we anxiously lament that we have offended You, and we condemn ourselves and our faults with true repentance, asking You to aid and deliver us by Your grace.

Draw near, then, O most gracious and most merciful God and Father, bestowing Your mercy upon us in the name of Jesus Christ Your Son our Lord. Removing our faults, and washing away all our pollutions, daily increase to us the grace of Your Holy Spirit, that we from our inmost hearts acknowledging our iniquity, may be more and more displeasing to ourselves, and so moved to true repentance, and that by purging us from all our sins, may He produce in us the fruits of righteousness and holiness pleasing to You, through Jesus Christ our Lord. Amen.

ASSURANCE OF PARDON

'For God so loved the world that he gave his only begotten Son, that whoever believes in him should not perish but have everlasting life' (*Jn. 3:16*).

'For the Son of Man has come to seek and save that which was lost' (Lk. 19:10).

'Jesus said, … "Son, be of good cheer; your sins are forgiven."' (Matt. 9:2).

'Therefore, being justified by faith, we have peace with God through our Lord Jesus Christ, … For when we were still without strength, in due time Christ died for the ungodly. … God commends his love towards us, in that while we were still sinners, Christ died for us. Much more then, being now justified by his blood, we shall be saved from wrath through him' (Rom. 5:1, 6, 8–9).

PSALM 121
(*Book of Praise: Anglo-Genevan Psalter*)

Unto the hills I lift my eyes.
From where comes all my aid
When troubled or afraid?
The LORD shall to my help arise,
He who made earth and heaven:
His aid is freely given.

2 Your Keeper slumbers not, nor shall
He cause your foot to fail
When dangers you assail.
Lo, he who keeps His Israel
Will neither sleep nor slumber:
Nought shall your life encumber.

3 The LORD your Keeper is for aye,
A shade on your right hand:
You shall securely stand.
The moon by night, the sun by day
Shall not afflict or smite you,
But with their radiance light you.

4 The LORD will guard and keep you when
You meet with harm or strife:
He will preserve your life.
When going out or coming in,
The LORD will you deliver
From this time forth, for ever.

PRAYER FOR ENLIGHTENMENT
(*the pastor chooses appropriate words*)

THE WORD OF GOD
(*The Geneva Bible*)

Also we know that all things work together for the best unto them that love God, even to them that are called of his purpose. For those which he knew before, he also predestinated to be made like to the image of his Son, that he might be the firstborn among many brethren. Moreover, whom he predestinated, them also he called, and whom he called, them also he justified, and whom he justified, them he also glorified. What shall we then say to these things? If God be on our side, who can be against us? Who spared not his own Son, but gave him for us all to death, how shall he not with him give us all things also? Who shall lay anything to the charge of God's chosen? it is God that justifieth. Who shall condemn? it is Christ which is dead: yea, or rather, which is risen again, who is also at the right hand of God, and maketh request also for us. Who shall separate us from the love of Christ? shall tribulation or anguish, or persecution, or famine, or nakedness, or peril, or sword? As it is written, For thy sake we are killed all day long: we are counted as sheep for the slaughter: Nevertheless, in all these things we are more than conquerors through him that loved us. For I am persuaded that neither death, nor life, nor angels, nor principalities, nor powers, nor things present, nor things to come, Nor height, nor depth, nor any other creature, shall be able to separate us from the love of God, which is in Christ Jesus our Lord.

(*Romans 8:28–39*)

PRAYER OF INTERCESSION
(all following in their minds)

Almighty God, heavenly Father, You have promised us that You will listen to the prayers which we pour forth to You in the name of your beloved Son, Jesus Christ our Lord; and we have been taught by Him and by His apostles to assemble ourselves together in one place in His name, with the promise that He will be present with us to intercede for us with You, and obtain for us whatever we shall, with one consent, ask of You on earth.

You teach us to pray first for those whom You have appointed to be our rulers and governors, and next to draw near and ask You for all things which are necessary for Your people, and so for all people. Therefore trusting in Your holy commands and promises, now that we have come into Your presence, having assembled in the name of Your Son our Lord Jesus Christ, we humbly and earnestly beg of You, O God, our most gracious Father, in the name of Him who is our only Saviour and Mediator, that of Your boundless mercy You would be pleased to pardon our sins, and so draw our thoughts to Yourself with full assurance, that we may be able to invoke You from our inmost heart, framing our desires in accordance with Your perfect will.

We therefore pour out our prayers before You, O heavenly Father, on behalf of all rulers and magistrates, whose service You employ in governing us, and especially for [our national Government and local Council], that You would be pleased to impart to them more and more every day of Your Spirit, who alone is wise and good, in truth the *highest* wisdom and the *chief* good, so that feeling fully convinced that Jesus Christ Your Son, our Lord, is King of kings and Lord of lords, just as You have given Him all power in heaven and on earth, so they too may in their office have a regard for His authority and the extension of His kingdom, governing all citizens as well as Your people (who are the work of Your hands and the sheep of Your pasture) according to Your will, so that we, enjoying stable peace both locally and throughout the nation, and in every other part of the world, may serve You with all holiness and purity, and, freed from the fear of our enemies, have cause to celebrate Your praise during the whole period of our lives.

Next, O faithful Father and Saviour, we commend to You in our prayers all whom You have appointed pastors over Your faithful people, and to whose guidance You have committed our souls; whom You have been pleased to make the dispensers of Your holy gospel; that You would guide them by Your Holy Spirit, and so make them true and faithful ministers of Your glory, making it their constant study, and directing all their endeavours to gather together all the weak and vulnerable sheep which are still wandering astray, and bring them back to Jesus Christ the chief Shepherd and Overseer of their souls; and that they may increase in righteousness and holiness every day; that in the meanwhile You would be pleased to rescue all churches from the evil designs of self-seeking religious leaders, who are led only by a love of power, fame or financial gain, and plainly have no concern for the manifestation of Your glory, and the salvation of Your flock.

Moreover, we offer up our prayers unto You, O most gracious God and most merciful Father, for all people in general, that as You are pleased to be acknowledged the Saviour of the whole human race by the redemption accomplished by Jesus Christ Your Son, so those who are still strangers to the knowledge of Him, and immersed in darkness, and held captive by ignorance and error, may, by Your Holy Spirit shining upon them, and by Your gospel sounding in their ears, be brought back to the right way of salvation, which consists in knowing You the true God and Jesus Christ whom You have sent. We beg that those on whom You have kindly bestowed the favour of Your grace, and whose minds You have already enlightened by the knowledge of Your word, may daily profit more and more, being enriched with Your spiritual blessings, so that we may all together, with one heart and mouth, worship You, and pay due honour, and yield true and loyal service to Your Son, Jesus Christ, our Lord, and King, and Lawgiver.

Furthermore, O Author of all consolation, we commend to You all whom you permit to suffer in various ways: those afflicted by war, famine, plague and other disasters; individuals also pressed by poverty, or imprisonment, or disease, or exile, or any suffering in body or mind, that wisely considering that the end which You have in view is to bring the disobedient back into the right path of Your will, may they be inspired with the sense of Your merciful love revealed in the Gospel, and repent with sincere purpose of heart, so as to turn to You with their whole mind, and being turned, receive full consolation, and be delivered from all their evils.

In particular, we commend to You our suffering brothers and sisters who live under persecuting regimes, and who are deprived of the liberty of openly calling upon Your name, and who have been either cast into prison or are oppressed by the enemies of the gospel in other ways. O merciful Father, kindly and tenderly support them by the strength of Your Spirit, so that they may never despair, but constantly persevere in faithful witness to You and Your truth. Be pleased to stretch out Your hand to them, aiding them in their distress. Console them in their adversity, and taking them under Your protection, defend them from their cruel persecutors; uphold them with all the courage of Your Holy Spirit, that their life and death may alike tend to Your glory.

Lastly, O God and Father, attend to the supplications of us Your children. We have assembled in the name of Your Son Jesus, for the sake of His word and of His Holy Supper. Being conscious of our corrupt nature, may we at the same time reflect how greatly we deserve condemnation. For we further realise how much we add to our guilt every day by our selfishness and disobedience. Since we recognise that we are devoid of spiritual purity, and that our flesh and blood are plainly averse to valuing our privileges and appreciating the inheritance of Your kingdom, may we with full purpose of heart and firm confidence devote ourselves to Your beloved Son, Jesus Christ, our Lord and only Saviour and Redeemer; that He, dwelling in us, may efface our old Adam and renew and transform us to a better life; that thus Your name, as it excels in holiness and dignity, may be honoured in every region and in every place. Amen.

THE LORD'S PRAYER
(original version or expanded form)

HYMN
(Ten Commandments: Book of Praise:
Anglo-Genevan Psalter, hymn 7)

CONFESSION OF FAITH

I believe in God the Father Almighty, Creator of heaven and earth.

I believe in Jesus Christ, His only-begotten Son, our Lord; He was conceived by the Holy Spirit, born of the virgin Mary; He was condemned under Pontius Pilate, He suffered upon the cross, feeling the torments of hell; He died and was buried; on the third day He arose from the dead; He ascended into heaven, and sits at the right hand of God the Father Almighty; from there He will come to judge the living and the dead.

I believe in the Holy Spirit; I acknowledge a Holy, Universal, Apostolic and Reformed Church; I believe in the communion of saints, the forgiveness of sins, the resurrection of the body and the life everlasting. Amen.

PRAYER OF PREPARATION

As our Lord Jesus Christ, not content with having once offered His body and blood upon the cross for the forgiveness of our sins, has also supplied them to us as nourishment for eternal life, so grant us of Your goodness, that we may receive this great blessing with true sincerity of mind and heart, and endued with sure faith, enjoy together His body and blood, even His entire person, just as He Himself, while He is true God and man, is truly the holy bread of heaven that gives us life, that we may no longer live for ourselves, driven by sinful self-will, which is altogether shameful, but He may live in us, and conduct us to a holy, happy, and everlasting life, thus making us truly partakers of the new and eternal covenant, even the covenant of grace; and in feeling fully persuaded that You are pleased to be for ever a just and gracious

Father to us, by not imputing to us our offences, providing us, as Your dear children and heirs, with all things necessary as well for the soul as the body, we may offer You endless praise and thanks, and render Your name glorious both by words and deeds. Enable us then, on this day, thus to celebrate the happy remembrance of Your Son: grant also that we may thoughtfully and joyfully proclaim the benefits of His death, and by receiving new increase and strength for faith and every other good work, we may with greater confidence profess ourselves Your children, and glory in You our Father.

THE LORD'S SUPPER
(Book of Praise: Anglo-Genevan Psalter)

PRAYER OF THANKSGIVING

We offer You immortal praise and thanks, O heavenly Father, for the great blessing You have conferred upon us unworthy sinners, in bringing us to partake of Your Son Jesus Christ, whom You purposed to be delivered to death for us, and now impart to us as the food of everlasting life. And now, may Your goodness towards us continue. Never allow us to become forgetful of these things, but grant rather, that carrying them about engraved on our hearts, we may profit and increase in a faith which may bear fruit in every good work. Thus may we dedicate the remainder of our life to the advancement of Your glory and the welfare of our neighbours, through the same Jesus Christ Your Son, who, in the unity of the Holy Spirit, lives with You and reigns for ever. Amen.

THE WORD PREACHED
(sermon constructed from the writings of John Calvin)

Introduction

The salvation brought by Christ is common to the whole human race, inasmuch as Christ, the author of salvation, is descended from Adam, the common father of us all (*Institutes, II. xiii. 3*). First, we must understand that as long as Christ remains outside of us, and we are separated from him, all that he has suffered and done for the salvation of the human race remains useless and of no value for us (*Institutes, III. i. 1*).

I

It is true that St John says generally, that [God] loved the world. And why? For Jesus Christ offers himself generally to all men without exception to be their redeemer ... Thus we see three degrees of the love that God has shown us in our Lord Jesus Christ. The first is in respect of the redemption that was purchased in the person of him that gave himself to death for us, and became accursed to reconcile us to God his Father. That is the first degree of love, which extends to all men, inasmuch as Jesus Christ reaches out his arms to call and allure all men both great and small, and to win them to him. But there is a special love for those to whom the gospel is preached: which is that God testifies to them that he will make them partakers of the benefit that was purchased for them by the death and passion of his Son. And forasmuch as we be of that number, therefore we are double bound already to our God: here are two bonds which hold us as it were [closely] tied to him. Now let us come to the third bond, which depends upon the third love that God shows us: which is that he not only causes the gospel to be preached to us, but also makes us to feel the power thereof, so as we know him to be our Father and Saviour, not doubting but that our sins are forgiven us for our Lord Jesus Christ's sake, who brings us the gift of the Holy Spirit, to reform us after his own image.

True it is that the effect of [Christ's] death comes not to the whole world. Nevertheless, forasmuch as it is not in us to discern between the righteous and the sinners that go to destruction, but that Jesus Christ has suffered his death and passion as well for them as for us, therefore it behoves us to labour to bring every man to salvation, that the grace of our Lord Jesus Christ may be available to them (*Sermons on Job*).

Christ ... was offered as our Saviour ... Christ brought life because the heavenly Father does not wish the human race that He loves to perish ... But we should remember ... that the secret love in which our heavenly Father embraced us to Himself is, since it flows from His eternal good pleasure, precedent to all other causes; but the grace which He wants to be testified to us and by which we are stirred to the hope of salvation, begins with the reconciliation provided through Christ ... Thus before we can have any feeling of His Fatherly kindness, the blood of Christ must intercede to reconcile God to us ... And He has used a general term [whosoever], both to invite indiscriminately all to share in life and to cut off every excuse from unbelievers. Such is also the significance of the term 'world' which He had used before. For although there is nothing in the world deserving of God's favour, He nevertheless shows He is favourable to the whole world when He calls all without exception to the faith of Christ, which is indeed an entry into life (*Comment on John 3:16*).

II

Christ ... offers salvation to all indiscriminately and stretches out His arms to embrace all, that all may be the more encouraged to repent. And yet He heightens by an important detail the crime of rejecting an invitation so kind and gracious; for it is as if He had said: 'See, I have come to call all; and forgetting the role of judge, my one aim is to attract and rescue from destruction those who already seem doubly ruined.' Hence no man is condemned for despising the Gospel save he who spurns the lovely news of salvation and deliberately decides to bring destruction on himself (*Comment on John 12:47*).

Moreover, let us remember that although life is promised generally to all who believe in Christ, faith is not common to all. Christ is open to all and displayed to all, but God opens the eyes only of the elect that they may seek Him by faith ... And whenever our sins press hard on us, whenever Satan would drive us to despair, we must hold up this shield, that God does not want us to be overwhelmed in everlasting destruction, for He has ordained His Son to be the Saviour of the world (*Comment on John 3:16, cont*).

This is His wondrous love towards the human race, that He desires all men to be saved, and is prepared to bring even the perishing to safety ... It could be asked here, if God does not want any to perish, why do so many in fact perish? My reply is that no mention is made here of the secret decree of God by which the wicked are doomed to their own ruin, but only of His loving-kindness as it is made known to us in the Gospel. There God stretches out His hand to all alike, but He only grasps those (in such a way as to lead to Himself) whom He has chosen before the foundation of the world (*Comment on 2 Peter 3:9*).

III

Since it is of very great importance to us to be so thoroughly persuaded of the fatherly love of God, that we continue to glory in it without fear, Paul cites the price of our reconciliation in order to confirm God's favours towards us. It is a notable and shining proof of His inestimable love that the Father did not hesitate to bestow His Son for our salvation. Paul therefore draws his argument from the greater to the less—since He had nothing dearer, more precious, or more excellent than His Son, He will neglect nothing which He foresees will be profitable to us. This passage ought to admonish and arouse us to consider what Christ brings to us with Himself, for as He is a pledge of God's boundless love towards us, so He has not been sent to us void of blessings or empty-handed, but filled with all heavenly treasures, so that those who possess Him may not want anything that is necessary for their complete happiness (*Comment on Romans 8:32*).

I approve of the common reading [of Isaiah 53:11], that He alone bore the punishment of many, because the guilt of the whole world was laid upon Him. It is evident from other passages ... that 'many' sometimes denotes 'all' ... That, then, is how our Lord Jesus bore the sins and iniquities of many. But in fact, this word 'many' is often as good as equivalent to 'all'. And indeed, our Lord Jesus was offered to all the world. For it is not speaking of three or four when it says: 'God so loved the world, that He spared not His only Son.' But yet we must notice what the Evangelist adds in this passage: 'That whosoever believes in Him shall not perish but obtain eternal life.' Our Lord Jesus suffered for all and there is neither great nor small who is not inexcusable today, for we can obtain salvation in Him. Unbelievers who turn away from Him and who deprive themselves of Him by their malice are today doubly culpable. For how will they excuse their ingratitude in not receiving the blessing in which they could share by faith? And let us realize that if we come flocking to our Lord Jesus Christ, we shall not hinder one another and prevent Him being sufficient for each of us ... Let us not fear to come to Him in great numbers, and each one of us bring his neighbours, seeing that He is sufficient to save us all (*Sermons on Isaiah 53*).

Let us fall down before the face of our good God ... that it may please Him to grant His grace, not only to us, but also to all people and nations of the earth, bringing back all poor ignorant souls from the miserable bondage of error and darkness, to the right way of salvation (*Calvin's usual end of sermon prayer*).

HYMN

Dedicated to Calvin & the Huguenots,
and all who suffer for Christ in every age.
Words by A. C. Clifford, based on Romans 8.
Tune: Psalm 68 (*Anglo-Genevan Psalter*)

ALMIGHTY Father, Lord and King,
Your suffering saints unite to sing
With holy jubilation!
We worship now before your throne,
Rejoicing since we are your own
By merciful adoption;
Predestined to behold your face,
Chosen to know such matchless grace,
Our souls rejoice with trembling;
Confiding in your sovereign power,
We are secure from hour to hour,
For God, our God, is reigning!

2 Almighty Saviour, Son divine
In whom the Father's glories shine,
Accept our adoration;
Holy Redeemer, you have died,
We by your blood are justified,
Freed from all condemnation!
Jesus, our Prophet, Priest and King,

Your ransomed ones rejoice to sing,
Despite our tribulation;
We conquer through your mighty love,
We have the victory from above,
Blest by your intercession.

3 Almighty Spirit, by your breath
All God's elect are raised from death;
Blessèd regeneration!
Spirit of Christ, come reign within,
Subdue we pray, our every sin,
Receive our supplication;
Help us in our infirmity,
Strengthen the sons of liberty;
In earnest expectation,
May we with joy, and patiently,
Wait for the glory yet to be,
Assured of our redemption!

FINAL PRAYER

(John Calvin)

GRANT, Almighty God, that since we are here exposed to so many evils, which suddenly arise like violent tempests,—O grant, that with hearts raised up to heaven, we may yet acquiesce in Your hidden providence, and be so tossed here and there, according to the judgement of our flesh, as yet to remain fixed in this truth, which You would have us to believe—that all things are governed by You, and that nothing takes place except through Your will, so that in the greatest confusions, we may always clearly see Your hand, and that Your counsel is altogether right, and perfectly and singularly wise and just; and may we ever call upon You and flee to this port—that we are tossed here and there in order that You may nevertheless always sustain us by Your hand until we shall at length be received into that blessed rest which has been procured for us by the blood of Your only-begotten Son. Amen.

BLESSING

The Lord bless you, and keep you: the Lord make his face shine upon you, and be gracious unto you: the Lord lift up his countenance upon you, and give you peace (*Numb. 6:24–6*). Amen.

This Liturgy is based on an edition of John Calvin's Genevan liturgy *La Forme des prières et chantz ecclésiastiques* (1542) by the Author, Norwich Reformed Church (August, 2002).

Huguenot Cross

THE HUGUENOT CROSS AND ITS MEANING

A variant of the Maltese cross was the basis of an insignia—the Order of the Holy Spirit—awarded by the French kings to soldiers and statesmen. A further Huguenot variation was made popular by a Protestant jeweller from Nîmes in the late seventeenth century. It became associated with the Huguenots and their sufferings in the post-revocation period. In time, the following interpretations became attached to it:

1. The Huguenots claimed the symbol (with slight variation) as Frenchmen and as 'soldiers of Christ'.

2. The four branches of the cross became emblems of the four Gospels.

3. The eight points of the cross came to symbolize the Beatitudes (Matthew 5:1–12)—marks of the true people of God.

4. The crown of thorns expresses the Huguenots' identification with Christ in all their persecutions and martyrdoms.

5. The four heart-shapes between the crown of thorns and the centre of the cross depict the hearts of God's people centred upon Christ alone for salvation.

6. The dove speaks of the Holy Spirit, the strength and comfort of God's elect in their pilgrimage to the glory everlasting.

"GOD MUST WIN"
(John Calvin to the faithful in France, 1559)